ONE GIRL
AND THE WAINWRIGHTS

ONE GIRL
AND THE WAINWRIGHTS

Eleanor Matthews

Published by Sigma Leisure – an imprint of
Sigma Press, Stobart House, Pontyclerc, Penybanc Road, Ammanford, Carmarthenshire SA18 3HP.

British Library Cataloguing in Publication Data
A CIP record for this book is available from the British Library.

ISBN: 978-1-85058-997-6

Typesetting and Design by: Sigma Press, Ammanford.

Cover photograph: Helm Crag reflections from the shores of Grasmere
© Eleanor Matthews

Photographs: © Eleanor Matthews

Printed by: TJ International Ltd

Quotes from *Pictorial Guides to the Lakeland Fells* by Alfred Wainwright, published by Frances Lincoln Ltd, © 2005. Reproduced by permission of Frances Lincoln Ltd.

CONTENTS

For Mum and Dad.
Thank-you.

Acknowledgments

First and foremost, my warmest thanks go to The Wordsworth Trust for employing me as an intern, enabling me to live in the beautiful Lake District and explore the fells to my heart's content.

To Elizabeth Jacklin, Joanne Marlor, Rosie Fearon and Bryony Matthews – getting soaked, cold, and exhausted in your company was definitely worth it! Long may the laughter, fun, and walking continue. Thank-you for allowing me to include your names and write about our escapades (I hope they won't prove too embarrassing for all parties involved).

I would like to thank my publisher, Sigma Press, for taking a chance on this particular hiker and supporting me throughout the strange world of outdoors publishing. My thanks also go to Frances Lincoln Ltd., for granting me permission to use and quote from Alfred Wainwright's *Pictorial Guides: The Eastern Fells*, *The Far Eastern Fells*, *The Central Fells*, *The Southern Fells*, *The Northern Fells*, *The North Western Fells* and *The Western Fells*, by Alfred Wainwright, 50th Anniversary Editions, published by Frances Lincoln Ltd, copyright © 2005.

Finally, for the bottomless encouragement, endless support, vast quantities of petrol, and unceasing interest in my quest to walk all two hundred and fourteen of the Wainwrights and write about them afterwards, I would like to give my greatest thanks to my Mum and Dad. Without you I'd still be working my way through the list...

INTRODUCTION

Forty Two is the number of Wainwrights that I have left to summit as I begin to write this book. I think of it as a momentous number with which to start off the year (a year in which I hope to finish ascending all two hundred and fourteen of the fells named in Alfred Wainwright's seven *Pictorial Guides to the Lakeland Fells*). A number any Douglas Adams fan would be thrilled to see at the top of this page, and a number that, for me, does indeed begin to hold the preciousness of life, the universe, and everything.

Let me begin at the beginning. I did not intentionally set out to 'bag' all of the Wainwright fells (snorts of derision, insert here). But it is true. Whilst growing up I have always been fortunate to enjoy long drives and days out with my family around the North York Moors, Yorkshire Dales, and Peak District, admiring scenery, visiting castles and stately homes and going for fish and chips more times than I can shake a stick at. A combination of this and hearing stories of my parents doing such walks as the Lyke Wake Walk, Yorkshire Three Peaks, Bow Fell, Scafell Pike, and the Pennine Way culminated in a long held desire to be one of those people who head off the beaten track and go where cars can't. I have always been a fan of camping, and have been on many camping expeditions with my dad, to places including the Isle of Mull, the Shetland Islands, the Lake District, and Fort

William (where we climbed Ben Nevis). I then and there decided to conquer all of the Munros, but that's another story... To swiftly move through the chapters of my life so far, in 2011 I moved up to the hallowed turf of the Lake District to work, where my love for fell walking truly began.

Life in the Lake District is surreal. Or at least, it is for me. From taking part in the Grasmere rushbearing celebrations to swimming in the lake, dancing in village hall ceilidhs and working with some of the most precious literary manuscripts in the English language, life in Grasmere is always changing. To live, however briefly, in a place visited by thousands of people each year who are escaping cities and urban life is a magical experience. To welcome them to Dove Cottage and show them proudly round, telling stories and jokes as we moved from room to room was a complete joy. Even if that joy sometimes involved a rainy day in the middle of August with dripping umbrellas, arguing families and hosts of bustling Japanese tourists who needed a translated tour (alas I am not fluent in Japanese – we had a recorded audio tour for them) all trying to enter the cottage at the same time. At the end of one particular Japanese tour, an elderly gentleman held out his hand to me and gently placed in my palm a beautifully crafted origami crane. The crane is a treasured keepsake, and lives in one of my desk drawers. I channelled the spirit of the Romantic poet William Wordsworth and his sister Dorothy by walking the fells, enjoying the picturesque, and exploring my surroundings.

One could consider Grasmere, where I lived, perfectly situated to begin fell walking, with all of the areas of the Lakes spread out around it like a spider's web. Grasmere is the arachnid in the middle, deciding which strand to explore on any particular day. My first few walks were centred around notable features near to the village – Grasmere Lake, Easedale Tarn, and Alcock Tarn. I wanted to explore further. Luckily there were a few other colleagues who were also interested in fell walking. On the twenty first of April in the year two thousand and eleven, after a day of work, EJ and I ascended Silver How together. We took sandwiches for our tea, and sat looking over the lake and the simply stunning view. It was my first Wainwright – but I did not know that at the time.

A week and a half later on a sunshine-filled May morning, I spent a few glorious hours climbing Helm Crag (and before anybody asks, no I didn't scale the Howitzer – as Wainwright never did, I don't think that it's necessary. However, I do intend to climb it one day!) Up until this moment, I knew a little of Wainwright and his fells, and had watched the television series in which a selection of them are climbed. I knew that Helm Crag was one of the fells mentioned in Wainwright's books. Later that day, on the way back from my triumphant conquering of Helm Crag, I bought a copy of the *Central Fells* from the newsagent's in Grasmere, primarily because I wanted to walk up Helvellyn and knew that Wainwright wrote about the different routes one could take. It will be no surprise to many readers of this book that Helvellyn is not in the *Central Fells* book, but in the *Eastern Fells*. However, it came as quite a big surprise to me. What was this book doing, not having Grasmere as the centre of the (roughly) circular Lake District? Why did the Dunmail Raise split up the centre of my Lakeland world? I was, however, excited to discover that Silver How was also a 'Wainwright'.

The *Eastern Fells* was duly bought. I immersed myself in the text and pictures and my imagination was hooked. The sheer number of fells! And their multitude of names – some sublime, some silly. And the fells which I had never heard of – Thunacar Knott, Saint Sunday Crag, Blea Rigg, High Tove, Ullscarf. Little did I think that I would eventually hold clear memories about each and every one, some fair, some foul. But all definitely worth it! It was at that moment that I formulated the plan of walking and climbing all of Wainwright's two hundred and fourteen fells. It seemed a task of epic proportions. Nevertheless I realised that living in Grasmere was a huge advantage as I was already well within the Lake District without having to travel to get here! I will never forget chatting to a gentleman on top of High Pike in the Northern fells, admiring the view of the back o' Blencathra and talking about the Wainwrights. He was also attempting to walk them all, only he was based in Devon. He commented how lucky I was to be based in Grasmere. I did indeed feel lucky.

For me, the initial attraction and plan to begin 'bagging' Wainwrights was not the ambition to climb a specific number of fells and see them ticked off a list (although I admit that it was gratifying to see the targeted 214 coming ever closer). The real appeal was the thought that, by trying to walk all of the fells described in the *Pictorial Guides* I would be forcing myself out of my little comfort zone around Grasmere. By having a target, I would not be tempted into walking the same few favourite fells over and over and over again (although I admit I did have many afternoon and evening strolls to both Alcock and Easedale Tarns). I would encounter parts of the Lake District and fells that previously had only been specks on the horizon. Through this, I would generate a deeper knowledge and understanding of the geography of Lakeland, and really make the most of living within the heart of the Lake District. I wanted to feel that I was really exploring, and get to know the fells and their quirks and personalities. I wanted to have conversations with other walkers and know what it is like atop of Sharp Edge, and not feel that I was missing out by not walking over Striding and Swirral Edges in the classic round from Glenridding. I wanted to revel in the solitude of the fells back o' Skiddaw and Blencathra. I wanted to have my own fireside tales of mud and bog and sunshine and snow. And by walking the Wainwrights, I felt that I would be very close to achieving that ambition.

Whilst undertaking my fell walking journey, I read many books about walking the Wainwrights. What struck me most of all was that all of these books were written by people who had walked the fells for years before adding to the Wainwright canon. Each time I walked a Wainwright, it was a new fell and a new experience. Furthermore, the vast majority of authors were all men. Where were the women writing about walking the Wainwrights? Is fell walking a more masculine pursuit? It was a combination of the desire to share my own perspective of walking the Wainwrights (both as a newcomer to fell walking and a newcomer to the Lake District) and to show that girls too love fell walking that I decided to write this book. It also came as a striking coincidence that I began fell walking in Lakeland at the age of twenty three – the same age that Alfred Wainwright himself came to the Lake District in 1930 and ascended Orrest Head, his first fell, near Windermere.

This book is not intended to be a guidebook to the two hundred and fourteen fells described in Alfred Wainwright's seven *Pictorial Guides to the Lakeland Fells.* It is – like Wainwright – my own love letter to the fells and the memories they have given me so far. I hope that you will enjoy hearing my version of what could be considered one of the most iconic of fell walking challenges. I hope that you will laugh at my escapades and shake your head at my misfortunes. But most of all I hope it will encourage you to go out and do the same. The fells are waiting for you!

Eleanor Matthews

THE FIRST FIFTY

Silver How was an unexpected struggle. It was meant to be a spontaneous evening stroll up a local fell with sandwiches in our rucksacks. I considered myself fit, and at only one thousand, two hundred and ninety two feet it should have been easy, right? We set off from Grasmere, walking through the village, past the lake, and onto the fell side. We followed the wall along, aiming for the gully and direct route up to the summit. Our first mistake was that we overshot the gully by some way before doubling back on ourselves, eventually finding the pitched stone staircase which takes you up the gully. From there it is but a short stroll to Silver How's summit. The second mistake was walking too fast. I am embarrassed to admit that I got stitch about half way up, and had to pause many times before collapsing in a heap next to the cairn. Nevertheless, I was proud of my achievement. After years of university pizzas and unhealthy student snacking, I had climbed a small mountain. The sandwiches were devoured with gusto. We descended by Wray Gill, passing Allan Bank on the way before returning home with starry eyes and tired limbs.

I look back on that walk with great affection, considering that only a few weeks later we climbed Helvellyn with no trouble at all. But it was the view that stands out in my memory the most. The whole vale of Grasmere stretched out before us with lights twinkling and lake water

The Howitzer (or one of its many aliases)

rippling. The weather was bright but cool, with a soft breeze. Mountains stretched for miles in all directions, and the feeling of freedom and possibility were unparalleled. It was there that I decided to climb all of the mountains that I could see, and once I discovered that Silver How was a Wainwright, my walking world was changed forever. Indeed every time I walked to the local shop, strolled across the lane to work, or came back from an evening in the pub, Silver How was there, encouraging me to keep going in my quest. I agree, Mr. Wainwright. Silver How is indeed a lovely fell.

Helm Crag is instantly recognisable. Looming up from Grasmere, I'm sure it is pointed out by every car which is driven along the A591 in either direction. It's summit has many names: the Lion and the Lamb, the Old Lady Playing the Piano, and the Howitzer. That morning, I woke up and – after peeping through my curtains – saw that the day was to be sunny and bright. Today's the day, I thought, I'll head up Helm Crag. I'd admired it many times, and was eager to see what it was like. I decided to ascend not by the usual route, but to walk partially along the Easedale Valley and climb up the fellside to Bracken Hause, thereby arriving at Helm Crag by the 'back door'. This meant that I would have the expansive view stretching before me as I descended via the popular route. As I set off, the day got hotter. And hotter. By the time I crawled up the flank of Helm Crag towards Bracken Hause I was positively melting. I spotted a tree halfway up and hallucinated that it was an ice-cream van – anything to persuade my sweaty limbs to make it to the ridge! Upon reaching the summit I plonked myself down and watched a man fail to climb the Howitzer. After a furtive glance around I propped my rucksack against the rock and attempted it myself. It may have been hot, but there was quite a wind on the summit. With my arms finding tiny ledges to grip and my legs swinging around wildly below for a firm hold, I abandoned hope and sheepishly retreated, resolving to climb it another day (as I'm sure many have resolved before me). As I prepared to leave the rocky summit behind, a young child raced past me and swarmed straight to the top of the Howitzer. Outshone by a ten-year old. Never mind. It was only later that evening that I learnt another lesson about the Wainwrights – always wear suncream.

One day at work, EJ and I were debating how quick it could take us to climb Helm Crag if we really pushed ourselves. We estimated that from leaving our house we might make it to the summit within an hour. And in true pioneer fashion, we decided to attempt it that very night. We hastened home, donned our gear, and marched off into the early evening. I am happy to announce that we made it up in exactly fifty nine minutes. Mind you, our legs were jelly by the time we reached the ridge and any thoughts of trying for the Howitzer had evaporated half way up the climb. The weather was cloudy but there was no rain, and as we were acting as latter day pioneers we carried on along the ridge to Gibson Knott, which at around eight o'clock that evening became my third Wainwright. By this time, the light was fading and we beat a retreat back the way we came, descending from Bracken Hause towards the Greenburn Valley and coming out onto the main road by the Traveller's Rest pub. Although we were well prepared and had torches in our rucksacks to use if necessary, it was a strange feeling walking home in semi-darkness. Gibson Knott thus reminded us of another lesson – make sure you have enough light to see by. Our lateness did have its rewards, though, for on the way home we stood and watched a beautiful Roe deer having an evening snack in a field just outside the village.

Despite having only completed three Wainwrights, my ambition to climb them all was firmly entrenched. I was eager to go out walking almost every day that I could escape from work, and wanted to introduce others to the joys of the fells. During the late May Bank Holiday weekend, my sister, B, came to stay and I persuaded her to walk over the ridge from Grasmere to Elterwater. We set off up Red Bank lane, and as we ascended out of the woods and over the top the weather worsened. It did not merely rain, oh no. The sky hurled buckets of water at us, precisely from the direction in which we were walking. We battled on against the elements. At one point, my sister shouted out that water was pouring down her sleeves. "Fasten your cuffs, then!" I yelled back through the rain. Another lesson learnt there: be sure to know your clothing. We eventually made it into Elterwater, where unbeknownst to B our parents were waiting and a pub lunch was calling. After drying out (the direction of the rain meant that the front of our clothing was saturated yet the back was dry) we went on a drive around the Lakes up the Honister Pass, where we visited the slate mine. After a drive past Buttermere, we headed up the Newlands Pass and stopped at Newlands Hause. Tantalisingly, a further Wainwright sits next to the small car park at Newlands. It was an opportunity Knott to be missed! (I apologise in advance, as terrible puns are likely to be a feature of this book).

Knott Rigg, when walked from Newlands, is an easily attainable fell if the conditions are right. The weather was right (glorious sunshine) but the wind was wrong (ferocious gale). As we ascended, we stopped walking, and started crawling along the ground like a crab. Two other small groups assumed similar stances, clutching the turf as a means of anchoring down against the wind. Part way up, my sister abandoned hope and turned back down the hill, clutching her hat in hand lest it should blow away and never be seen again. She promised to catch me if I rolled downhill. I pressed on upwards. To my shame, two hillwalkers with four trekking poles between them strode past me as if the vicious wind was a gentle summer breeze. Aha, I thought. Those be experienced fell wanderers, ready for anything Mother Nature can blow at them. I planned to get myself one of those strange stick contraptions, as they seemed marvellous things. Eventually I hauled myself to the summit and quickly made my way down the mountain, unaided by the wind which still tried to knock me off my feet. Back at the car park, day trippers were eating ice-cream, oblivious to the plight of those who still slogged up the hill. Knott Rigg therefore taught me another rule: do not be fooled by appearances. It may look calm and sunny, but be prepared for anything. The Boy Scouts have certainly got that one right.

Despite the elements, that same evening proved to be bright and sunny, and once again we were out on the fells, albeit this time much closer to home. Loughrigg Fell was our objective, and it proved to be a simple and enjoyable meander along the terrace and up to the trig point. It felt wonderful to look at the view and admire the fells which I had previously climbed. Unfortunately I had forgotten about poor B, for when I turned around she was sitting on the ground, looking tired and red from exertion. Within my first few weeks of fell walking in the Lakes I had already learnt more about how to walk than in all my years watching survival programmes on television. Another lesson, then: recognise your companions and be sympathetic of their ability.

To be fair, B had previously walked the Inca Trail and been to Machu Picchu, so I'm sure she was only a little out of practice. However, B was to suffer again at the hands of my Wainwright journey, but not until the very final walk to claim my two hundred and fourteenth Wainwright, which was possibly the most difficult mountain of all.

If you have been noting the order in which I began to climb the Wainwrights, you may have seen that my early focus was the fells which immediately surround the vale of Grasmere. Therefore, you have probably guessed that my attention soon turned towards those fells to the east of the village, the most prominent of which is Stone Arthur. Ever since I was a small child I have been a bookworm, and a trip to the local library was a joyous occasion. I am fascinated by all words, rhymes, poetry, and prose. Consequently, it will come as no surprise that I studied English literature at university, with my specialism being Medieval literature, particularly Arthurian literature and Middle English romances. To see a fell that was possibly named after King Arthur, and which had an alternative name of Arthur's Chair was incredible. I had to go! Arthur's Pike, near Ullswater, held a similar fascination, but it was a few months before I managed to walk there. Where does the name come from? If anybody has an inkling, please let me know as I would be very interested in finding out more.

The day came when it was time to release the Medieval knight within me and go on a quest to Stone Arthur and beyond! I made my way past the Swan Hotel, where Sir Walter Scott used to sneak in for an early morning drink whilst staying with the Romantic poet William Wordsworth. Following the route up Greenhead Gill, I approached the summit and perched on Arthur's Chair, surveying my own precious kingdom of Grasmere. The day was bright and clear, and I chose to see where my feet would take me. I walked uphill to Great Rigg, which has a sprawling cairn. Understandably, I did not leave it there, but moved onwards to the famous mists of Fairfield, which fortunately were not misty. I imagine that the summit plateau would be a very confusing place to be in mist, so best to be avoided, just in case. The summit is very expansive with a fantastic view down the horseshoe towards Lake Windermere and quite a few cairns are dotted here and there. I went to all of them and startled one lady who quickly pulled her trousers up as I appeared – the call of nature is understandable, but I would have picked a more secluded spot, not the summit of one of the most popular mountains in the Lake District! Especially as Fairfield's summit was very busy when I arrived, with people arriving and leaving in all sorts of directions. A troupe of young men jogged across the summit, paused briefly, the leader shouted triumphantly "On to Dollywaggon, lads!" and they were off again down the steep scree path towards Grisedale Tarn.

Over the years, I have heard much about that same scree path that goes up to Fairfield from Grisedale Tarn. In his younger days, my dad used to go walking all over the country, sometimes taking my mum with him. On one occasion, they were youth hostelling in the Lake District, and planned to walk from Grasmere to Patterdale via Grisedale Tarn, Fairfield, and St. Sunday Crag. The walk was progressing well, and halfway up the scree path to Fairfield they stopped for a rest.

"Come on, then", said my dad, "it's time to move on."
"No" was the response.
"What?"
"I'm not going up any more."
"Ok, then we'll go down", reasoned my dad. If my mum wasn't happy with going up, then there was always the alternative path along the Grisedale valley floor.
"No, I'm not going down either."

This posed a tricky problem. Nervous of the moving scree and the feeling under her boots, my mum refused to move for quite some time. After some coaxing, they eventually made it to the top of Fairfield and followed their intended route. Upon recent questioning, mum assures me that there must have been much more scree back then than there is now, and that it was her one and only hiccup during years of walking. Nevertheless it has proved an amusing anecdote in our house for many years.

After my exploration of Fairfield, I had three choices. Do I return the way I had come, walk along the western arm of the Fairfield Horseshoe, or do I go along the eastern arm? Three, two, one, time is up. I chose the western arm, retraced my steps to Great Rigg, and strode along the ridge to Heron Pike, which is distinctly lacking in herons. I found the summit quite hard to pick out, but Wainwright usefully distinguished it by pointing out the quartz in the rock. I saw, I bagged, I conquered (to paraphrase slightly). Nab Scar duly followed, with quite an arduous descent to Rydal which makes your knees ache. Walking past Rydal Mount, a former home of William Wordsworth, it's impossible to ignore the bookish connections, with Wordsworth, Coleridge, Walter Scott, and Southey frequenting the area. The day had been quite a literary walk, beginning with medieval literature and ending with Romanticism, a theme which pleased me no end. I hadn't set out to walk from Stone Arthur to Fairfield and back across to Nab Scar, but one of the great joys of fell walking is that it allows for spontaneity. Spontaneity which, despite my weary limbs, led me into Grasmere that evening to the annual village ceilidh, where we danced and reeled and capered throughout the evening.

As you can imagine, my desire to properly finish the Fairfield Horseshoe was soon satiated, as later that week JM and I followed the

Literary Lakeland strikes again!

same route up to Fairfield (by way of Stone Arthur and Great Rigg), and continued on to Hart Crag. En route to Dove Crag we attempted to find the Priest's Hole, which is a cave that offers good shelter and has a guidebook inside for visitors to sign. However, despite our best efforts, the day was moving on and so too must we. One day I'm sure I'll find it. Dove Crag is a gentle name for a fell, but there were no doves. It is amazing how many Lakeland fells are named after animals that don't live anywhere near the fell – Dove Crag, Eel Crag, Calf Crag, Hen Comb, Eagle Crag, to name just a few examples. We may as well include any Pike within that list, for I never saw any floundering fish upon Heron Pike's mountain tops.

When standing upon Dove Crag, we were in a quandary. Visibility was good, and we could see Little Hart Crag in the distance. To bag, or not bag? That was the question posed to us. It didn't look too far away (famous last words). To bag, was the decision we made. We were in good spirits, and began our descent. Being novice hill walkers, we didn't realise that nine hundred feet of descent and re-ascent towards the end of an already fairly long day would prove trying. Upon reaching Little Hart Crag, we summitted the fell and admired its lion-like shape, posing as a guardian to the larger fells around it. The sun retreated and we silently contemplated the walk back up to Dove Crag. It seemed a long way away. Nevertheless we enjoyed the detour, although the long pull up the flank of Dove Crag was tiring. It is always interesting to read about the order in which people walk the Wainwrights, to see if any forward planning and strategy was used. At the start of my journey, I generally did whichever fells I fancied, in no particular order. Had I been more strategic, I would have left Little Hart Crag until another time, as I passed over it again later in the year when walking from Middle Dodd to High Hartsop Dodd. But more on that walk later. Back to the Fairfield Horseshoe.

When we saw an impressive cairn in the distance as we were heading for High Pike, we presumed it must be High Pike and we duly made a beeline towards it. I have no idea why we thought this, and it was only when we got to the real High Pike that we realised the imposter was High Bakestones. Nevertheless it was a good imposter, with a wonderful view down to the Scandale Valley and Little Hart Crag where we had just been. The last Wainwright of the day was Low Pike, which we almost missed as the summit is squished onto an outcrop next to a dry stone wall. A satisfying descent into Ambleside marked my completion of the Fairfield Horseshoe. A gentle jog to the bus stop did not dampen our spirits, but the rain did.

Seat Sandal is a hulking fell, rising up from the Dunmail Raise like a sleeping leviathan. As it happened, the very next day the weather forecast promised sunshine. I cast my mind to fells around Grasmere which could be reached on foot without the need for a bus to take me to my start point. Seat Sandal seemed a likely fell. My choice of ascent route was via Little Tongue Gill and the eastern flank along the wall. Boy, was it steep. At the summit, I decided to recline against the fell, have a little morsel of something to eat, and revel in the silence and stillness of the day. It did not last long. As I was sitting quietly, I heard the patter of four feet hastening towards me. An energetic Border Collie dog bounded up to me, and began barking. Not the bark of a happy and content dog, but the urgent bark of an anxious one. I petted the dog. I gave him some of my sandwich. The dog barked on, jumping up around me. Running footsteps soon followed the dog, this time a human.

"Are you alright?" the lady asked with a concerned expression.
"Yes, thank-you – I'm just enjoying my sandwiches and having a rest, admiring the view."
"You're not hurt or distressed in any way?"
"No, no, I'm fine, but the dog seems a little overexcited."
"She would be – she's a trainee search and rescue dog. She's learning to bark like that when she finds a casualty out on the fells."

As it turns out, the collie had bounded up the fell, seen me, presumed I was in trouble and summoned his owner. It's good to know that the search and rescue dogs are trained so thoroughly, and hope that this one makes it into the ranks who go out in search of fell walkers who *really* need rescuing. Within this Seat Sandal story lies a lesson for us all. When enjoying a contemplative moment up on the fells, don't sit too still or you will be mistaken for a casualty who needs to be rescued!

It was eleven o'clock in the morning, and the day was warming up. I can only blame the exuberance of youth for the continuation of my walk that day. I descended down the gentle western slopes to the Dunmail Raise, crossed the road, and headed up the nose of Steel Fell. This was to be an up-and-down sort of day. Steel Fell was cruel to me that day, as it has quite a few false summits before the true summit of the fell is reached, and on a hot day the horseflies were out in abundance, which added to my discomfort. I then followed the ridge route around to Calf Crag. It was much later that I read that the ridge route I had chosen was notoriously marshy and boggy. This proved to be quite true. As I strode confidently along the ridge connecting Steel Fell and Calf Crag, something unexpected happened. The ground ate my foot. More specifically, my left foot disappeared into a patch of thick black bog, until I couldn't see below my ankle. This was highly disconcerting, and was my first encounter with bog (it was not to be my last). As I pulled my foot out the suction strength was so strong that as my foot – with walking boot thankfully still attached – emerged from the gloop I promptly fell on my bum into another area of bog. Let us say that I was very relieved to reach the summit of Calf Crag. My mood soon picked up on the descent down the Far Easedale valley, which is supremely beautiful. However, it soon dipped when I realised that I had run out of water. The supplies I had brought were not adequate for the extension of my planned route. However, I had almost reached Grasmere village when I realised this and so it was not a problem. For all future walks I made sure I had more than enough to last throughout the day.

There are four fells in the Lake District which extend up into the clouds and over the hallowed milestone of three thousand feet. These are Scafell Pike, Skiddaw, Scafell, and Helvellyn. It was Helvellyn that I was most eager to climb, as I had viewed it from afar on many occasions. EJ and I planned our route carefully, with the intention to ascend via Grisedale Tarn and climb Dollywaggon Pike, Nethermost Pike, Helvellyn, White Side, and Raise. Descent was to be down the Sticks Pass and then catch a bus back to Grasmere. The day started off well. We soon encountered our first obstacle, with the bridge over Tongue Gill being closed for repair. Rather than continuing on alongside Little Tongue Gill, we found some makeshift stepping stones to cross the water, and continued along the eastern side as planned. Grisedale Tarn was, as ever, supremely beautiful, and EJ resolved to come again another time to do some sketching. The zig zag track up the side of

Dollywaggon Pike depleted our energy reserves, but we eventually emerged onto the plateau, increased our pace and walked straight past the summit without even seeing it. It was only after seeing a man rejoin our route from a slightly different path we realised we had bypassed the summit, and doubled back on ourselves. It was then the weather changed. What had previously been early June sunshine made a split second decision to hail on us. It was a race to don our waterproofs! Those hailstones were painful. Nethermost Pike was reached without incident. The hail had turn to rain, and I'm sure there was a brief flurry of snow before the rain came.

Standing on Helvellyn's summit, sunshine engulfed us once again (with a biting wind for company). There were hikers all over the place, coming from all different directions. I saw a line of people like ants marching in a row, all crawling over the cliff edge and up the path to the trig point. Where were these people appearing from, I thought? I wandered over for a closer look, and got my first ever view of Striding Edge. It was magnificent, a shark's tooth of a ridge running for just over a mile. It looked challenging. It looked exciting. It was like a siren's call to me, and I knew that one day I too would complete the famous Helvellyn circuit from Glenridding, ascending and descending along Striding and Swirral Edges. I walked back to EJ, and we hungrily consumed our packed lunches. The Romantic poet William Wordsworth climbed Helvellyn many times during his life, and I can understand why. It definitely deserved to have a poem written about it! Helvellyn is also a highly decorated fell with three memorials on and around its summit, and can also boast of hosting the first ever mountain top landing of a plane in the British Isles, which occurred in 1926.

An eerily creeping mist chased us off Helvellyn and down to White Side. It swooped after us in a menacing blanket of nothingness, and embraced us as we approached Raise. We soon reached Sticks Pass. Too soon – we did not want our day to end! As an encore, and as weather conditions had returned to normality, we decided to nip up Stybarrow Dodd and back down again to the Pass, making our steady way down to the road. The other Dodds looked inviting, but we knew our limits. On our descent we made friends with a Shetland pony, watched traffic being halted for some time whilst a herd of cows crossed the A591 road, and made our way to the bus stop. We consulted our timetables, and could not believe that we had missed the bus by five whole minutes. It would be at least another hour before the next one would come along. Never mind, we thought, there's a pub down the road, we'll have a drink whilst were waiting. However, there was no need to wet our whistle as the moment we began walking towards the pub what should round the bend but a double-decker bus. We jogged back, thumbed it down, and had a welcome rest as it meandered alongside Thirlmere back to the village. We definitely slept well that night.

My next planned hike did not turn out as smoothly as I had hoped. As a matter of fact, it is one of the very few walks I have done that made me feel disheartened with the mountains (indeed I can only think of one other walk that made me feel this way). It is not above me to admit that I've made a fair few navigational errors during my walking career thus far, and am happy to share with you my woes as well as my joys. It is not an understatement to say that Sergeant Man gave me one of my worst fell walking moments to date, one in which I fell apart. It is embarrassing to even contemplate sharing it in this book, but I hope newcomers to fell walkers will take heart that others have misfortunes when they start out, and that it shouldn't put you off fell walking in the future. Even now, with a few years of experience under my belt, I still get moments of uncertainty, or of wishing I had company to confirm my position. Coming back down from Sergeant Man I vowed never to go up again. So far, I never have.

I must have got out of the wrong side of bed that morning, as the day started innocently enough. I walked up to Easedale Tarn as I had done so a few times before, interest being provided by extensive path repairs just after crossing Easedale Gill. The tarn was, as always, beautiful. My problems started as I walked along the south side of the tarn. Instead of neatly side stepping a small area of boggy ground, for some strange reason I decided to try and jump over it. This did not prove successful. As I landed, one foot skidded and my whole body landed with a great thump in the bog. From hair to foot one side of me was now a black mess. I hastily got out some tissues and tried to wipe away the worst of the damage. I tried to call out a jaunty "Hello!" to two hikers who passed me, but could only manage a feeble squeak. For some reason my fall put me on edge, and I felt jumpy. With hindsight, I should have turned back and gone back to Grasmere as I knew I didn't really want to continue with the walk. Nevertheless I persisted, and for a short distance all went well. I reached a crossroads, of which I knew I had to veer north-west to reach Sergeant Man. The path seemed to go in this direction, so without examining my map I followed it. Upon reaching a tarn, I got very confused. I wasn't back at Easedale Tarn, so where was I? Readers familiar with the central Lake District will know that I had stumbled upon Codale Tarn, a site which is ideal for wild camping. I looked at the map, but there was no path marked to this tarn. I should have consulted Wainwright, who notes an alternative route to Sergeant Man via Codale Tarn. I didn't. Reader, I sat down by the tarn and tears came to my eyes. I became very upset and angry at myself that I had become lost. How would I live down the shame? I admit that all I wanted was to give up and go home.

I am pleased to say that I didn't. After exchanging taut greetings with a walker who looked at me curiously (I'm sure the red-rimmed eyes were a giveaway) and a distressed phone call to my dad who quite rightly told me to get a grip on myself, I persevered. I made it to Sergeant Man. I even made it to High Raise. I was triumphant! That day was another steep learning curve not to panic, but to calmly assess the situation. Of course, I was never in any real danger of becoming lost. I now know my route error could have been easily resolved by simply going back the way that I had come and rejoining the main route. I also know that I should have listened to myself and made Easedale Tarn the aim of the walk, not Sergeant Man. Instinct is a wonderful thing and should be heeded. Descent was a much happier affair – I was very glad to be off the fells – and even found some tadpoles frolicking in a pool of water.

Of the mountains described in Wainwright's *Pictorial Guides*, there are many smaller fells which do not fit easily into a long walk. It was early on in my quest that I decided to walk a few of these mini mountains together, combining them into groups which I would conquer in a single day. Luckily (or unluckily, depending on who you ask) I had a ready-made chauffeur who I could call upon. Dad, welcome to the limelight. I provided a list of six fells; you supplied the transport and worked out how to get to them. This is how I managed to climb Binsey,

Sale Fell, Ling Fell, Great Mell Fell, Little Mell Fell, and Gowbarrow Fell all in one day. The night before, I had danced the night away at a 1980s themed birthday party for one of my housemates. We made her a Rubick's Cube birthday cake. The next morning, I tiptoed around leftover legwarmers, abandoned neon necklaces and empty glasses to escape into the mountains.

Binsey is one of the Lone Rangers of the Lake District. It stands alone behind the Northern Fells, small and often abandoned in favour of the higher, grander mountains. Yet for a little effort you can gain a big reward. The views across to the Solway Firth and the wind farms of northern Cumbria are captivating, and beckon any walker to go further north and hike the Scottish hills. To the south Wainwright's *Northern Fells* spread out like a fan before you, waiting to be traversed. It is a perfect fell for young children, grandparents, and dogs. I am very fond of Binsey, despite spending relatively little time on it as I was up and down within half an hour. Why the rush, you might ask? At the risk of being labelled a hill bagger, I had more fells to hike that day, and needed to be on my way.

Some fells can be easily paired together to make twin walks. Sale Fell and Ling Fell are two such hills. I'm sure I'm not the only person who, when contemplating the pair of fells, have begun singing the famous song that comes to mind when you combine both 'Sale' and 'Ling'. My ascent of both began near Eskin, where a short, steep ascent of Sale Fell led me to the grassy summit. It had no cairn, just a flattish pile of shingly stones. Ling Fell was grassy too, with a dome like shape which Wainwright compares to a Christmas pudding. I took a circular route to the summit, following the corpse road around before spiralling in. A trig point marks the highest spot. Three fells down! Corpse roads were tracks used to carry coffins from remote communities to the nearest church or place of burial, and I have found them to be eminently useful on my travels around the Lakes. I often used to walk the Coffin Route from Grasmere to Ambleside as an alternative to catching the bus, especially in the height of summer.

Driving in to the Lake District along the A66 (where, as I am not in America, I get my kicks), heads are turned towards the right to Blencathra with its fabulous arêtes, ahead to Grisedale Pike and

Keswick, or left to Clough Head and the Dodds. If the two small lumps on the landscape receive any acknowledgement at all, it is a fleeting glance before the mind turns back to the more 'exciting' fells. Yet Great Mell Fell and Little Mell Fell are better than their reputation deserves. Yes, they are small. Yes, it takes less than an hour to ascend and descend each one. Yes, there are other mountains which boast better ridges and rockier summits. However, Great Mell Fell is 'great'. I am a huge admirer of the trees on the fell, which have been blown and stripped and twisted by nature into weird and wonderful shapes which Wainwright describes as 'grotesque'. Witches, goblins, elves and trolls can be found in the shape of the branches, and would be a fascinating place for children to explore. Danger used to lurk here too, with the presence of a disused rifle range prompting a cautious lookout for flying bullets (the range may be defunct, but it's better to be safe than sorry...). Similarly, Little Mell Fell is convenient for a steep and quick jaunt to a summit that can be achieved in less than half an hour, with a good viewpoint to the south west. At this point in the day I was beginning to tire, the drizzle had set in, and I had just one more walk to complete before we headed home.

Gowbarrow Fell is perfectly positioned next to Ullswater and the famous Aira Force waterfall. The poet William Wordsworth writes of the waterfall in his poetry, and it was near the shores of Ullswater that Wordsworth observed the daffodils referred to in his most famous poem. In April 1802, Wordsworth was out walking with his sister Dorothy in wet weather when they spotted a line of daffodils. She described their encounter in her journals, and Wordsworth was inspired by her musings to write the poem *I wandered lonely as a Cloud.* I wonder how many visitors to the famous Aira Force waterfall and the shores of Ullswater also take in Gowbarrow Fell. Certainly not many on the day I was there, for as I stepped onto the path that heads toward the memorial seat near Yew Crag, the rain became strong and everybody seemed to be heading back down to the car park. Despite this bad omen, I took the circuitous ascent around the crag to the ruined shooting lodge, following the peaty path to the attractive trig point summit. Views were minimal and the rain had increased, so I descended the same way. However, I did allow myself a detour to admire the beautiful Aira Force, which is an impressive sight as it crashes sixty five feet down a ravine.

It is a truth universally acknowledged that there will be some Wainwrights of which I write lots about, and others of which I write little. On some fells I had adventures, on others I didn't. High Rigg was one of the latter. Situated near the pretty little church of St. John's-in-the-Vale, I dashed up and down High Rigg in the pouring rain. It is, however, one of the smaller fells which I think deserves a repeat visit, as its central position suggests that the view on a clear day would be fantastic. The day that I climbed High Rigg was another day of 'ticking off' a group of unrelated fells. I intensely dislike the phrase 'ticking off' as it implies that the walk is merely a means to an end (the end in this case being the achievement of walking all of the Wainwrights). Whilst it was immensely satisfying to work my way through the list of Wainwrights, it was the list that was the means to my end – my end being a greater understanding and appreciation of the Lake District. Wainwright provided the framework to my exploration of the Lakes. Walla Crag was the next fell to contribute to this, and my choice of ascent to the summit was from Rakefoot. What a summit! It definitely rivals Surprise View as a lookout point. A rocky platform poking out above Great Wood from which picturesque Derwentwater and Bassenthwaite can be viewed. Fells opposite include Catbells, a firm family favourite, and Maiden Moor – all of this from a fell which is only one thousand, two hundred and thirty four feet in height! My visit was made all the more special due to the weather, which changed from moody mist to shining sunshine in the space of a few moments and the view opened up before me in slow motion. It is amazing how quickly the weather can change (you'll remember how changeable it was during my ascent of Helvellyn, where sun, snow and hail welcomed us to the mountains). As they say in Scotland, if you don't like the weather all you have to do is wait five minutes.

My final fells that day were Latrigg, Grange Fell and Hallin Fell. Wainwright certainly knew how to pick his peaks, as Latrigg is as gentle as Yewbarrow is fierce. A short stroll is all that is needed to reach the flat summit and the extensive view. On a clear day even the heady heights of Scafell Pike and Great Gable can be seen. Driving back down the road towards Keswick, we were greeted by a group of five wild guinea fowl. They jostled across in front of the car and made a dash into nearby greenery. Continuing my traverse of today's chocolate box selection of fells (some you love, some you don't) we drove down a scenic road which ends in the pretty village of Watendlath. Watendlath is notable for being the location for the Herries series of novels by Sir Hugh Walpole. If you are familiar with this area of the Lake District and read the novels, his descriptions of eighteenth-century Cumberland are strikingly accurate. Back to Grange Fell. At this stage in the day, wherever I looked, mist was coming ever closer and enveloping the hill tops as it moved. It was a race against time to conquer Grange Fell before I couldn't see anything at all. This proved harder than I had imagined. I followed the path ascending from Watendlath, which Wainwright notes as being straightforward and 'dull and damp'. Dull and damp it was, but straightforward it was not. I lost the path and was forced to meander this way and that to avoid suspicious looking patches of ground before I happened upon a sheep track which led me to the summit, which is called Brund Fell. To this day I'm only ninety nine percent certain that I reached the true summit of Grange Fell. That said, I'm not yet prepared to return to satisfy that one percent. My boots became saturated with boggy water, and my feet squelched with every step.

Hallin Fell was the final fell of the day, and was another quick and steep jaunt, this time at the eastern side of Ullswater, near Howtown. The giant obelisk on the summit is a particular favourite cairn of mine with a spectacular view of snaking Ullswater. On my descent, I passed the gruesome skeleton of a long-gone sheep, the bones bleached white. I am happy that my journey to complete the Wainwrights did not end for me like it did for the sheep.

There are many great horseshoe walks within the Lake District. If I asked you to tell me some, the Fairfield Horseshoe would spring to mind, perhaps alongside the Mosedale Round, the Coledale Horseshoe and the Newlands Round. There are even some in Wainwright's *The Outlying Fells of Lakeland*, such as the Bannisdale Horseshoe – I have by no means named them all. One of the largest horseshoe rounds in the Lakes which takes in a number of Wainwright summits (the number can increase or decrease depending on which fells you include) is the Kentmere Horseshoe. It is a horseshoe that I was really looking forward to completing, as it would be my longest walk to date in an area I hadn't ventured into before.

My chosen route was to extend the usual horseshoe and add in a fell or two to increase my tally for the day. Any reader who has been to Kentmere will know that it is tucked away up a beautiful valley and is fairly time-consuming to reach, even without the 'will there or won't there be a parking space' question hanging over your head, so I wanted to make it worth my while. The plan was to walk clockwise from Kentmere, taking in Yoke, Ill Bell, Froswick, Thornthwaite Crag, Gray Crag, High Street, Mardale Ill Bell, Harter Fell, Kentmere Pike, and Shipman Knotts (in that order). I definitely cut my teeth on long distance walking that day. Walking up the Garburn Pass, I passed the Badger Rock (a favourite with boulderers) and began my ascent along the ridge. It has many ups and downs and is quite rocky underfoot, making the walk an exciting traverse into the heart of Wainwright's *Far Eastern Fells.* I was in a glorious mood which wasn't dampened when wind blew up and the rain blew in when I reached Yoke. A bad weather front was moving in from the west, which set in for a few fells until I reached High Street. Ill Bell has three tall cairns, making it a particularly memorable fell – they act as the three guardians of the summit. By contrast, Froswick is seemingly insignificant when compared to its near neighbours, yet has a distinct character of its own, gentle and powerful. It also has an excellent view of the Kentmere Reservoir. Froswick was also the first fell on which I spotted the ubiquitous orange peel left on the ground by a careless visitor to the summit. Yes, it is biodegradable, but is still an unsightly mess. Take all your rubbish home, please! That includes you too, banana peel fiends. Thornthwaite Crag's beacon stands like a landmark for miles around, drawing you in like moths to a candle.

My first real detour from the Kentmere Horseshoe came when I veered off to Gray Crag. It added an hour to my journey but was definitely worth it as I couldn't really join it to any other fells in another walk. Surprisingly, Ullswater and the Helvellyn fells were very clear in the distance, despite the rain. It was a tiring detour, for although the re-ascent was not much, it lasted for quite some distance! After what seemed like an age but was in reality probably about an hour I reached the half way point in my walk – the marvellous High Street. Wide enough to not only have a Roman road running across it, but also expansive enough for those selfsame Romans to race horses on it. Racecourse Hill is a wide grassy plain which could give Ascot or

Newmarket a run for their money. Alas I was not feeling energetic enough to do my best gallop to the concrete trig point, so tried a sedate trot instead.

High Street, home of Roman soldiers and racehorses

Unusually, I had the normally popular High Street to myself for twenty glorious minutes. After consuming my jam sandwiches with gusto, two women came along to say hello and garnish the cairn with a stone or two. They too were doing a horseshoe, but told me they were making it up as they went along because they knew the area well, and so didn't need to bring a map. This is a rather silly prospect, for even if you know the fells inside out, a thick blanket of mist can alter perspective and confuse very easily. I wished them luck, and was on my way. Mardale Ill Bell is perhaps overshadowed by its near neighbour, High Street, yet has a rather impressive view of Small Water and Haweswater. However, I admit I hastened onwards quickly, as I knew the last sharp ascent of the day was just around the corner. The summit of Harter Fell is reached after conquering the final steep pull of the day. Let us say I was thankful to reach the top!

Harter Fell is perfectly positioned between two of the Lake District's most famous packhorse routes – the Nan Bield Pass and the Gatescarth Pass – and so bad weather alternatives are present if the weather proves really rough. Like the cairn on Starling Dodd, Harter Fell's summit decoration is a writhing mass of metal and stone. Wainwright's description of it as nightmarish was quite correct! As I followed the ridge and fence along to Kentmere Pike, I admired the other side of the horseshoe where I began earlier that day. It seemed so long ago! As I photographed myself by the trig point, there was a definite feeling of satisfaction that this was the penultimate summit of the horseshoe. The final summit, Shipman Knotts, had a puny cairn consisting of a few limp and apologetic stones which do not do justice to the fact that it was only at this point that the full extent of the Kentmere Horseshoe was revealed to my gaze. Strolling down into Kentmere I was visited by a final shower of rain which dampened my waterproof coat, but not my spirits.

There are occasions when out fell walking where one can only assume that a temporary fit of madness can explain your actions. Therefore I can offer no explanation other than the exuberance of youth when, straight after completing the Kentmere Horseshoe, I was a glutton for punishment and walked up Dodd. Oh no, you cry! Dodd is one of the northern fells, you can't possibly be telling the truth. But I am. My parents had a hankering to see the ospreys nesting at Bassenthwaite, and so they walked up to the viewing area to spy on the birds whilst I ascended Dodd, following the circular gravel path to the summit. The summit of Dodd is now one of my favourite viewpoints in the Lakes, with delights such as Derwentwater, Bassenthwaite, the Newlands Valley and the Isle of Man all visible. Much of the extensive forestation that Wainwright wrote of has been removed at the summit, making Dodd an attractive reward after so short a walk. I would recommend visiting it in the early evening when the shadows are lengthening along the valley floors. Eleven fells in one day – I would not better that tally throughout the rest of my journey to complete the Wainwrights.

Some fells were created to be enjoyed by the masses, and others to be savoured by the few. Wansfell was destined to be enjoyed by the masses, primarily due to its proximity to Ambleside and Stockghyll Force waterfall, which was a great favourite with Victorian tourists. On a sunny July day the fell was to prove just as busy as in its Victorian heyday. The weather was muggy as I approached Stock Ghyll lane and began to climb the stone pitched path. I then proceeded to pass, in order, a group of approximately twenty Germans, three sets of families, a group of Boy Scouts, and lots of couples who were wearing jeans. It was a relief to have the rocky top of Wansfell Pike to myself. Aha, you say! The true summit is not Wansfell Pike, but Baystones further along the ridge. It is indeed, and I strolled along the ridge to the summit, making friends with wild horses en route. It rained on the summit, and stopped raining as I departed. Typical. As I ambled down to Ambleside I passed through the old revolving gate and had a look at Stockghyll Force. It's definitely worth making a short detour to see, for although it is not as impressive as Aira Force, it is quaint and set in lovely leafy grounds.

After Wansfell, I caught the bus to Windermere and made my pilgrimage to the summit of Orrest Head, which is the first fell Wainwright ever walked in the Lake District. It boasts a wonderful panorama over the fells and it is no wonder than Wainwright fell in love with Lakeland there and then. I was, however, disappointed to find that somebody had destroyed the sign on the viewing platform which identified all of the mountains in the distance, and replaced it with ugly broken bottles. I have since been pleased to learn that it has been replaced with a new sign which I hope lasts for many years. Whilst waiting in Windermere station to catch the bus back to Grasmere, I struck up a conversation with a lady from Kentucky who was going to camp that night and do a walk. She showed me her map and asked me what I thought it would be like camping on Dove Crag (which is part way round the Fairfield Horseshoe) because it "looked like a flat area". As it was now three o'clock in the afternoon and raining hard with ominous looking clouds in the distance, I tried to suggest that she stay in Ambleside that night and complete her walk tomorrow. This is because it would take her a number of hours to get to her destination, which is fairly exposed and made more dangerous in bad weather when the light would be poor and she would be tired.

She 'ummed' and 'ahhed' and decided that she would start walking the "trail" and find a nice place to camp on the walk regardless of the weather conditions. I wished her good luck, and hoped that she was successful! There were no accounts of a missing American on the news that night, so I hope she found a decent camping site around Ambleside.

There are some fells which catch your eye again and again, yet you never seem to get around to climbing them. St. Sunday Crag was one of these fells. A shapely dome like the hump of a sleeping dragon, St. Sunday should be proud that such a mountain bears his name. Having got to know the route from Grasmere to Grisedale Tarn fairly well by now, I chose to begin my ascent of St. Sunday Crag by that route, taking the diagonal slanting path up to Deepdale Hause and on to the summit. Despite its steep-sided appearance, the summit of St. Sunday is remarkably flat. Nevertheless, I was pleased that such a mountain was my fiftieth Wainwright. The sky was brilliantly clear with not a cloud in the sky (it was July after all, but then summer does not necessarily mean sunshine in the Lake District). After admiring the view from St. Sunday Crag, my focus turned to Birks.

COMPANIONS

I take much pleasure in walking alone. When fell walking by myself, I can pause when I like, eat when I like, change route on a whim, explore where I like, and walk for as long or as short a length of time as I like. I can compose poetry as I walk. I can sing at the top of my lungs with only a Herdwick sheep to hear. On the many occasions that I have seen snakes of five, ten, or even twenty ramblers I shy away from them. When forced to pass them I follow Wainwright's example - one or two hellos will do for the whole group. While descending from my third attempt at reaching the summit of Wetherlam I counted no less than forty three people ascending Coniston Old Man in

A constant companion who never complained or talked too much — my shadow

one long conga line. I'm sure the Old Man would have liked this in his Young Man days. Nowadays he prefers the sheep.

However, despite all appearances, I do enjoy having company on my walks, and have enjoyed the companionship of different people throughout my quest for the two hundred and fourteen who have provided me with many laughs and smiles along the way. I've had support both on and off the mountains. When I moved to Grasmere, I could drive but did not have a car, and relied heavily upon the local bus service to take me further afield. When I wanted to walk in places that – lest you hire a private jet – are nigh on impossible to get there and back in a day by public transport, I hired a personal taxi service. This taxi service is otherwise known as the car of Mum and Dad. They often drove up to the Lake District, picked me up, dropped me off somewhere and at a prearranged time and place picked me up again. I got a brilliant day's walking; they got a lovely day trip to the Lakes. Everyone wins! Apart from the time I was four hours overdue and darkness was falling... I am tremendously grateful for their support, and know that I could not have completed the Wainwrights without them. Indeed, even on days where my legs were stiff from the day before and I wanted to do nothing but curl up inside a duvet, make like a dormouse and sleep, my dad would be trawling through the list of Wainwrights, suggesting ones which I should tackle next.

I often walked with strangers who I met on the fells and with whom I exchanged tales of mountain days before parting. We shared conversations of joy, history and dreams. Some people scuttled past me quickly with barely a glance of acknowledgment, clearly wanting to retreat into solitude. Some tried too hard to be good companions. Numerous awkward silences have been experienced by one joke too far, or no joke at all. I climbed Helvellyn for the first time with EJ, via Grisedale Tarn, Dollywaggon Pike, and Nethermost Pike. On the way up, we had the widest variation of weather conditions you could ask for – mist, sunshine, hail, and rain. A chap we got talking to on Nethermost Pike mentioned that when he put his shorts on, the farmers started to bring their sheep indoors! (No, we didn't think it was very funny either.) Unfortunately he said it straight after a rather ordinary comment about the spectacular view, and we were unprepared for his dazzling wit to strike. We didn't realise that it was a joke (summit fever, perhaps?) and an uncomfortable pause ensued whilst we assumed an expression of polite puzzlement. When he reached Helvellyn's cross-shelter a few minutes after us to retreat from the wind, he did not join us, but chose a different section. I wonder why...? Clearly he was disgruntled with our lack of appreciation of his mirth.

I took great pleasure in observing my fellow walkers. Tourists and residents alike roamed the hills. It was rare that I saw a sad face. Tired, angry, frustrated, maybe, but never sad. From the matching cagouled couples to the garishly clothed family, we fell wanderers are a strange breed. Of the larger groups, men almost certainly outnumbered the women. Dwarfing me with their outsized rucksacks, I was immensely proud that they needed to roam in packs and I strode out alone. Solo male walkers were plentiful, but I can recall meeting very few female lone walkers. I hope that the story of my Wainwright adventures will inspire others to go out and do the same.

I am not frightened of walking alone, although I have been asked time and again whether or not I feel safe, being a young girl alone in high places and not knowing who might be around the corner, behind a tree, or lurking in amongst some nearby boulders. Yet I have never been scared. I am aware of my surroundings, don't take risks, and have found other fell walkers – male and female – to be the same as me. We all love the countryside, are eager to explore it, and are happy to share it with like-minded people. I would wholeheartedly encourage other girls to walk however they feel comfortable, whether that be on your own, with friends, or in a group. Don't let fear of the unknown prevent you from wandering off the beaten track.

When finishing the Wainwrights, many completers take members of their family and groups of friends up their final fell, to turn it into a celebration. I took only one person – my sister, B – and she hated every minute of it. When her memory has faded into rose-tinted nostalgia, I expect she'll come walking with me again. At least, I hope that she will. For now, every time my two hundred and fourteenth fell is mentioned, all I get is a pair of glowering eyes and a muttered curse. Despite my best efforts, I also received glowering eyes and muttered curses (this time in German) from some other temporary companions

I unwillingly adopted whilst fell walking. When contouring around Rest Dodd heading for The Nab, I met a German couple who tailed me for a while before asking clarification on their position. I obliged, and they were dismayed to find that Rest Dodd was not The Knott, as they had thought (and which they were aiming for).

First they laughed, saying how I joked with them. Then they pitied me, saying that I must be mistaken as I was so young. Then they grew angry, saying that I was purposely misleading them and that I did not know what I was doing. I assured them that I knew exactly where I was, and as we had perfect visibility patiently showed the couple how the features on my map matched the real geographical features around us, explaining the route they should take. They did not have a compass with them, and had only a photocopied sheet of paper as a map. The day was moving on and I had to be finished and back down to Brothers Water within a few hours to get the last bus home. Eventually I left them arguing between themselves. My suggestion that they return the way they had come went unheard, and I left with the strains of irritated German floating after me on the breeze. I hope that they did eventually find The Knott and the way back down the mountain. I watched the news carefully that night, but as there was no mention of stranded tourists up in the Far Eastern Fells I presume they did the sensible thing and retreated. It wasn't the first time I'd offered advice to those who asked for it whilst on the fells, and it wasn't the last time it went unheeded, either.

Nature was a constant companion during my walks. The Herdwick sheep are undoubtedly a universal favourite. Their smiling faces and hardy (or should that be 'herdy'?) resilience in all weathers is definitely worthy of admiration. I spent quite some time wanting to stroke one before getting my chance. Enjoying a walk around Rydal Water one evening, I spotted my opportunity. After an exploration of Rydal caves, we were walking back along the terrace when a startled sheep jumped onto the path right in front of us. I darted forward, and managed to stroke the wiry wool before he ran away. After remembering about sheep ticks I slapped at my clothing and wriggled around, at last satisfied that I did not have an unwelcome companion aboard my body. One of my regular walking buddies, JM, was to have her own close encounter of a Herdy kind when walking along Greenup

Gill near Stonethwaite after descending Sergeant's Crag, and she too was delighted to feel the wool of a Herdwick.

Another iconic symbol of the Lake District is the red squirrel. Sadly endangered, these beautiful animals (it feels insulting to refer to them as rodents) have a stronghold in the Lake District National Park. I have been lucky enough to spot red squirrels three times. I'm sure plenty of my readers will have seen red squirrels before, but for those who haven't, I say put your boots on and get out there! Their tufty ears, cheeky faces, and bright colour can't be surpassed (sorry, Herdwicks). Each time I've seen a red squirrel I was on my way to conquer a Wainwright. Heading up to Skiddaw one perched on a fencepost, driving round to Mellbreak another ran across the road, and descending from Green Crag I had a standoff with a third near Doctor Bridge in Eskdale. Seeing them in their natural habitat and not on television are moments that I will treasure. Each time I saw a red squirrel I counted it as a lucky charm. This is in addition to a lucky charm I have worn whilst walking every single Wainwright – a Viking ship necklace obtained in the Shetland Islands on a camping holiday some years ago.

Inevitably, the friends who I lived with in Grasmere became embroiled within my walking quest. Some came walking with

Herdwick sheep. They are many. They are always watching you

Walking companions come in all shapes and sizes

me, some listened to my tales, and I'm sure all thought that I was ridiculously obsessed with the Lake District fells. Indeed some days I felt I had best not discuss my wonderful day of walking with the sun shining and sheep bleating, when my housemates had returned from a tiring day at work entertaining the day trippers who flock to Grasmere each year. On those occasions, I could be more often seen quietly writing in my diaries. Looking back through the information I scribbled down brings each step by wicked step back into vivid moving picture. I am a great person for diaries and mementos, and as such my notebooks are filled with bus passes, car park tickets and little tokens from my days on the fells.

One thing more (a vitally important point to mention!) is the reception my note-taking gained in my shared house in Grasmere. I lived with seven others in Town End. They soon became accustomed to the sight of me in our living room writing up my walks. It became a mark of honour, a badge of pride if you like, for my housemates to be featured by name in these notebooks. This meant that they had accompanied me on a walk! A running joke was that if I eventually – as I had long wanted to do – turned the detailed notes and tales in my diaries into a travelogue about walking the Wainwrights, then the housemates who were in them would get at least one mention. Therefore, as promised, Lizzie Jacklin, Joanne Marlor, and Rosie Fearon – I salute you. Well deserved! I hope you enjoy reminiscing about our walks in this book, and the memories that we have shared.

Whether you choose to walk alone or with companions, I hope that my experiences will encourage you to traverse the fells, create your own memories, and explore some of the best of British walking country. Everyone who completes the Wainwrights has their own story, and this book is mine.

THE SECOND FIFTY

Flat and unassuming, Birks is more often than not climbed as a result of its proximity to St. Sunday Crag, as I doubt that many walkers would choose to walk with Birks the main objective of the day. As I rested on its grassy summit and contemplated the rest of my walk, a man and a woman passed me, chatting between themselves. I could not help but overhear their conversation, which began with the woman uttering a profound statement.

"I can't see the summit."
"We're on the summit."
"Oh good, what mountain have we climbed again?"
"St. Sunday Crag."

St. Sunday Crag? We were all on Birks, and the hulk of St. Sunday loomed above us to the south west. I wondered at what point they would realise their mistake, or perhaps they wouldn't realise? They might climb St. Sunday Crag thinking it was Fairfield, and then when on Fairfield perhaps imagine it must be Helvellyn, and that the other limbs of the Fairfield Horseshoe were actually Striding and Swirral Edges. They might return triumphantly home wondering what all the fuss about Striding Edge is, as they managed it with no trouble at all. These two were definitely a pair of berks on Birks (I apologise once again for the terrible pun). I dearly wish I knew what they thought when they began to follow the path upwards towards the real St. Sunday Crag. Chuckling to myself, I moved on to my next target, Arnison Crag.

With hindsight, I should have followed the fence off Birks and around Trough Head, thus reaching Arnison Crag without an excessive amount of descent and re-ascent. Hindsight is a marvellous thing. Instead, I continued down over Thornhow End, followed the path around the base of the fell and ascended alongside the wall near Oxford Crag. Nevertheless I reached Arnison Crag with a little effort, and enjoyed the rocky summit immensely. The 'rock gateway' mentioned by Wainwright feels like a passageway between two parallel worlds. Upon reaching Patterdale, I then contemplated my return journey. As it was now midday the sun was beating down strongly and I didn't fancy a great deal of ups and downs, so plumped for the walk back along the Grisedale valley, following the path of Grisedale beck. The valley route is a particularly lovely one, and puts into perspective the scale of the mountains around you. I couldn't quite believe that a few hours earlier I had been on top of them, looking down to where I was now. Now it was me who was the small fry looking up at the giants.

As I set off homeward bound I passed the time of day with an elderly couple. I have often been pleasantly surprised by the friendliness of walkers in the Lake District, and this couple were no exception. They kindly offered to share a taxi back with me to Grasmere (as that is where they too were heading, although they were finishing their walking in Patterdale having walked along the valley from Grasmere). When I politely declined, assuring them that I had enough water and energy to last my return leg, they wished me well. The gentleman joked that, after all, I could afford to walk back to Grasmere as I was likely to live longer than them and so had more time! A sobering thought indeed.

The walk back was incredibly scenic, and although the sun was now scorching, I was in seventh heaven. Upon reaching Grisedale Tarn for the second time that day, I paused and looked around. I am glad that I did, as I noticed a metal sign glinting in the sunlight. It was the

Brothers' Parting Stone, which is a plaque and sign commemorating the spot where, on the 29th of September in 1800, the poet William Wordsworth saw his brother John for the last time. They didn't know it at the time, but John was to be shipwrecked when sailing on the *Earl of Abergavenny* in 1805. Canon Hardwicke Rawnsley, one of the founding members of the Wordsworth Trust, the National Trust, and a friend of Beatrix Potter, proposed that a stone and plaque be built in commemoration, which is the one that you see today. It is a little weather-beaten, but still evokes the emotional turbulence of the place. I made it home tired but triumphant. What a walk!

Despite lingering aversions to the path around Easedale Tarn as noted previously, I found myself up there once again not long after my epic Grisedale walk. My target this time was Tarn Crag. Having reached the tarn, I found a path which snaked upwards and around the crags, contouring around the lumps and bumps before reaching the summit. The view is rewarding for what seems like a small effort, with the tarn sparkling below and the Langdale Pikes poking up behind. As it was still early, the day was fine and I had no other plans, I felt as though I should try a little harder. Blea Rigg was selected as it was close by, and it has an even better view of the Langdale Pikes. I am pleased it had something going for it, for there was any number of confusing cairns atop of the rocky outcrops. They all looked to be of similar heights, so I visited them all, just in case. After some exploration I also discovered the Shelter Stone, and crammed myself inside it (you're not telling me that you wouldn't have a go, too?) A few walkers passed me and looked at me quizzically. It is rather snug, but handy to know that it is there if required in poor weather. I may have looked like a goblin hiding under a rock, but I felt like an adventurer!

Living in the Lake District, it doesn't take much persuasion to go out and climb the mountains that are all around you. Nevertheless it always surprised me how many of the people I knew showed no inclination to do just that. They would admire the fells from ground level, but not venture into the airy heights – unlike me, who willingly scrambled, hiked, and explored wherever possible. However, it was interesting to hear even those who had not hiked much mock Skiddaw as dull and tedious. Mighty Skiddaw, fourth highest mountain in the Lake District, tedious? Surely not. I had to investigate further. The morning after a party in our house which featured duelling wizards, a treasure hunt for magical talismans and an intricately crafted owl costume, others were nursing aching heads whilst I set off to see if these claims about poor Skiddaw were true. Starting at the Latrigg car park, I marched off up the 'tourist track'. An advantage of this popular route up Skiddaw is that the path is wide and unmistakeable. However, it is rather stony and feels like a motorway. Thus I took the first opportunity to branch out, following a minor path up the side of Whit Beck and made my way to Lonscale Fell. I turned to look up at Skiddaw and the predictable Lakeland Gods had changed the sunshine into clouds. As I began the walk toward Skiddaw Little Man and his more famous dad, it was like seeing the (quite literal) wool being pulled over their eyes as they acquired a cloud hat. I imagine the views from Skiddaw Little Man would be great – if only I could have seen them! The Little Man's cairn would have been an undistinguished slate pile, apart from the fact there was a single rusty piece of farming machinery on top. Wonders never cease!

Clouds of my own breath swirled in front of me as I trudged up to the summit ridge. All was silent and eerie, and it was reassuring to hear a shepherd in the distance round up his flock with hearty shouts. Two mountain bikers whizzed past me downhill at breakneck speed. I'm not sure I would want to drag a bike up to the summit of Skiddaw for a few minutes of adrenaline! The summit of Skiddaw itself was cold with a chilling wind. I studied the viewing plaque, despite there being no view. After a quick rest I navigated towards the steep, slanting scree path towards Carlside Tarn. After a bit of mind trickery in which I couldn't seem to find the cairn, I summitted Carl Side and headed down the ridge. Anybody who derides Skiddaw as lacking in adventure should try ascending via Longside Edge. It has fantastic views of Bassenthwaite and the northern fells, is narrow enough to feel adventurous, and even has a few short scrambles along the way. It is more challenging than the 'tourist track', so I would recommend it. Whilst walking down the ridge I claimed two more Wainwrights, Long Side and Ullock Pike. Turning back to look at Skiddaw it was mightily irritating to see the summit now completely clear of mist. You win some, you lose some. Never mind. On the descent I passed the group of stones called the 'Watches'. They would be more accurately called the 'Watch*ers*', as they crouch together like a secret society discussing devious plans. Today's walk also brought back memories of a childhood holiday to the Lake District, where we stayed at the nearby Ravenstone Hotel. My two main recollections of the holiday focus on this hotel. Firstly, I'm sure I spotted the actor who used to play Enid Blyton's Julian from *The Famous Five* television series in the 1990s walking down the stairs (if you don't recall this series, shame on you, it was 'smashing'!) Secondly, the hotel breakfast. I persuaded my parents to let me have kippers instead of the usual full English breakfast. I tried to eat them, but the bones! There must have been thousands of bones in my two kippers. I tried to pick them out but they kept getting stuck between my teeth. The Ravenstone are still serving up kippers for breakfast. I wonder if they are descendants of the ones I consumed? As you can see, the lure of the Lake District had been building from a young age.

Never one to miss an opportunity, when the suggestion came that (as it was still only midday and conditions were perfect) now might be a good time to stroll up a few of the smaller fells, I couldn't resist. Thus the same day that I tackled Skiddaw happened to be the same day that I made my first foray into Wainwright's seventh book, *The Western Fells*. A gentle ramble was to be had as I made my way around and up to the tops of Low Fell and Fellbarrow. There were lots of families on Low Fell that afternoon, which is not surprising as it is a very welcoming fell with exquisite views of Grasmoor and Crummock Water. I must have been unfortunate enough to come across a person who was having a rather bad day, for as I approached Low Fell's cairn I called a cheery hello to a chap sat at the cairn. He looked up at me, grunted, and shot off along the ridge. I was sorry I had interrupted his peace, but there was no need for rudeness! Fellbarrow too is a corker of a fell, with views across to the Isle of Man and Scotland on a clear day. Its prime position has been acknowledged by the geographical surveying clan, who built a trig point on its highest spot.

If you ever claim to be a Lakeland hiker who revels in steep ascents, arresting views, and long walks, sooner or later you will be asked what you think of the Langdale Pikes. I finally had my chance to form my own opinion on a scorching Sunday in July. The Langdales are a group of mountains which have such a distinctive shape that they are easily identified from a long distance. Driving down the A591 alongside

Windermere it became a tradition of mine to shout out "The Pikes, the Pikes!" as soon as they came into view. My choice of route will be similar to many who have climbed them. I began at the New Dungeon Ghyll Hotel, followed the route of Stickle Ghyll up to Stickle Tarn. From there, I made my way up to Pavey Ark, Thunacar Knott, Harrison Stickle, Pike o' Stickle, and Loft Crag, before descending along the Mark Gate path back to New Dungeon Ghyll. Stickle Ghyll was like a queue at a bank on market day, there were people everywhere! I can't complain though, as I did choose to be out on a busy summer weekend.

When I say that I 'made my way' up to the summit of Pavey Ark, I have to announce that I did not choose to go by way of Jack's Rake, but up the North Rake instead. I considered Jack's Rake from afar, but there was a queue of at least ten people waiting to climb it. As I didn't want to be stuck behind them (I prefer to keep moving) I chose an alternate route instead. It is not embarrassing to say that I was also a little wary of Jack's Rake reputation, as it has sadly been the cause of some deaths over the years.

The alternative North Rake was exciting too, as it is quite steep with some shifting scree always willing to upset your footing. The summit of Pavey Ark has a magnificent view, although I had to wait for some lingering cairn-hoggers to depart before I could gaze down onto the mesmerising Stickle Tarn. Thunacar Knott, I am sorry to say, is rather a bland fell – even the view is not up to par to usual Lakeland standards. In comparison, my next objective, (Harrison Stickle), had a magnificent three hundred and sixty degree panorama of fells which was breathtaking. I could see Helvellyn, Coniston Old Man, Scafell Pike, Skiddaw, Bowfell and the rest all with wonderfully crisp clarity. Harrison Stickle has three prominent cairns and I duly visited each of them. It was snided with people, as the whole of Kendal walking club had decided to lunch on the summit. I don't blame them! Similarly, I enjoyed Pike o' Stickle immensely, especially the scramble necessary to reach the summit. There is a great view of the Crinkles from Pike o' Stickle – I added that one to my mental list of 'Wainwrights I want to walk as soon as possible'. Sitting quietly, I was drinking in the view from the summit when two young men came up the path towards Pike o' Stickle.

"Where's the path gone?" one of them asked, confused.
"Mate, I think it's up there!" replied the other, pointing to where I sat lounging against a rock.
"Oh no", was the only response given. I think he may have been a little scared of heights (they did eventually make it to the summit though).

The final fell of the day, Loft Crag, was achieved by a short stroll, before what felt like a never-ending descent back down to New Dungeon Ghyll, where a thoroughly deserved steak pie was waiting for me. I was thrilled to have had enjoyed such a great weekend of walking, and a pie has never tasted so good.

The next week, I scanned the bus timetables carefully as I was in need of a walk which was covered by bus routes. I chose a trio of fells near the Kirkstone Pass which I could link together easily with the help of public transport. This was how, one early Friday morning, I could be seen toiling up 'The Struggle' from Ambleside. My plan was to walk up the road ('struggle' up the road would definitely be a more appropriate verb) and leave it to follow the ridge to the summit of Red Screes. The weather was cloudy and overcast, and drizzle chased me as I slogged up the fell. Some Lakeland features are unfortunately named and I am afraid that Snarker Pike has drawn one of the short straws. It may be more than bad luck which named it, however, as Red Screes has more than one false summit when you ascend from Ambleside, and Snarker Pike made many a snark and snide remark to me as my hopes rose and fell. Eventually Red Screes was summitted. There is, fairly unusually for Lakeland, a small tarn on the summit of the fell. Kirkstone Pass was a tiny grey snake far below me, with cars like ants whizzing back and forth. I could have ascended from the summit of the pass up the eastern side of the fell, but to me that was cheating!

I duly wandered down the Smallthwaite Band to the summit of Middle Dodd. It did feel odd to be descending to reach a summit. Beggars can't be choosers, however, and I was pleased to gain another Wainwright so swiftly. It was a pleasant stroll with a lovely view of Brothers Water, Place Fell, and Great Mell Fell to the north. I contoured back around Red Screes to cross the Scandale Pass to Little Hart Crag. Having already spent some time on the latter fell's summit previously whilst walking the Fairfield Horseshoe, I soon descended to the summit of my final fell of the day: High Hartsop Dodd. I followed the fell down its steep northern edge (which I consider to be the nose of Brothers Water) towards Hartsop Hall. High Hartsop Dodd is another pretty fell which looks very difficult when seen from ground level, but simple when viewed from above. Perspective is a marvellous thing! I rambled through farmers' fields to walk alongside Brothers Water. Brothers Water was originally called Broad Water until two brothers tragically drowned there in the nineteenth century. I felt like I had stepped back in time with the stillness of the area, the horseflies dancing round me, and a young shepherd training a sheepdog to round up a flock of sheep – definitely a pastoral idyll, especially as the sun had decided to put his hat on. After happily trundling around the lake, I caught the bus for what must be one of the most scenic bus journeys in England back to Windermere, and on to Grasmere.

Almost every time I go fell walking I take away a memory to be treasured and remembered on cold winter evenings when I wish the days were longer. However, there are some trips which surpass all others in terms of experiences, memories, and sheer fun. When combined into a two-day walking extravaganza where a heady mixture of excitement and fear are present, some walking trips simply cannot be beaten. Television programmes and newspapers are always citing the fact that more people are choosing to take a 'staycation' than a vacation. That summer, two friends and I decided we would do the same, and would walk our way around the Lake District.

The fun began. Where should we walk? How would we get there? Which area of the Lake District had we not explored yet? Wasdale, Ennerdale, Coniston, and Eskdale – all of these names were thrown into the mix. A major factor to consider was our lack of an automobile for the trip, and our reliance upon public transport. This ruled out Wasdale, Ennerdale, and Eskdale. Coniston was a strong possibility. I came across some boat timetables, and that opened up a whole new can of proverbial worms. How adventurous it would be to begin our trip sailing across a lake into the unknown! The north western fells would be our objective. We moved onto accommodation. It soon became clear that, until we became fully fledged adults with a wage to match, hotels (and even bed-and-breakfasts!) were far out of our price range. Youth hostels it was then. Despite the prevailing stereotype of European youth hostels being dens of vice, loose morals and petty theft, the youth hostels of England retain a pre-war innocence in the minds of many, with rambling, singsongs and hearty cheer being customary. Our plans were set, our chosen Lakeland youth hostel was booked, our bags were packed, and we eagerly waited to hit the fells. The three musketeers of EJ, JM, and I were ready to set out on a grand adventure.

The morning of the fourth of August arrived and it was raining cats and dogs outside. Nevertheless we kitted up, locked the door behind us, said goodbye to the sleepy hamlet of Town End and walked to the bus stop. The rain got even wetter and big drops bounced off the hood of our jackets. We donned our waterproof trousers and danced a sun dance to encourage the rain to stop. It did not. Eventually the bus arrived and we filed on, dripping onto the seats and steaming up the windows. The bus couldn't drive to Keswick fast enough for us. We were cutting it fine, for once at Keswick Bus Station we had a stiff walk across to the boat landings. With minutes to spare, we bought our tickets and clambered aboard the *Princess Margaret Rose*. 9.45am sharp she sailed across the lake, with us as her only passengers. Derwentwater was choppy and we felt like true explorers as we began our epic trip. Our first fell of the day loomed out of the cloud ahead of us: Catbells.

As we gazed up at Catbells, we conversed with the captain of the ship.

"Going walking, girls?" he began, talking in a strong Cumbrian accent. "Yes we are – our plan is to walk from Catbells to Buttermere along the fell tops."
"Looks nasty up there in the cloud. You know you shouldn't be going up there in this weather, could be dangerous."
"…"
"If you haven't done much walking, I think you should change your plans."
"…"

It would have been hard to explain that by now all three of us had experienced quite a lot of what the Lakeland fells could throw at us, and were confident that we were fully prepared for our trip. Nevertheless, his advice was kindly meant and we appreciated his concern. We disembarked at Hause End, said goodbye to *Princess Margaret Rose*, and set on our way.

Catbells is famous for being the home of Mrs Tiggy Winkle, Beatrix Potter's endearing character, and for being an all-round family friendly fell. We saw nothing of the hedgehog as we made our way up the nose of Catbells from Hause End, and no families either, for as we ascended our view of Derwentwater receded. We were firmly in the mist and thoroughly enjoying ourselves. It was rainy but warm and we alternated between jackets on and jackets off to try and get a happy medium. JM opted for a t-shirt and was much more comfortable than me in a waterproof coat! However, I was drier. Although seemingly innocent, Catbells does have one or two tricks up her sleeve, including a false summit which we looked at hopefully until the true summit reared its head behind. Additionally, the 'steep but obviously simple scramble' as observed by Wainwright would prove difficult to all but the most agile of grandmothers, especially when it is slick with rain. Nevertheless we gained the summit without mishap.

Maiden Moor is a beautiful and romantic name for a fell and a very pretty fell it is too, with heather and grass covering the summit plateau. Who knows which maiden gave her name to the mountain? In the mist and rain it was all too easy to imagine Ivanhoe riding a fine steed along the ridge towards us. I blame active imaginations for the fact that we had to double back to gain the summit cairn of Maiden Moor, as we missed it due to the mist. Nevertheless, our hearts and minds were strong and we galloped on to our next fell, High Spy, where victuals and repose awaited our hungry bellies and parched throats. I shall leave the inspiration of Sir Walter Scott behind, and move onto the realms of Ian Fleming.

If Maiden Moor conjures images of white knights and princesses awaiting rescue, then High Spy suggests a villain's secret hideout and place to spy on the good guys trying to stop them. For all we know, High Spy's summit cairn could contain a stone which, when pressed, reveals a door into the old mine workings and an evil den below. However, I shall stop my imagination from running away with me, and merely comment that the cairn on High Spy is very impressive, and there are plenty of stones nearby that make handy seats at lunchtime. Indeed, when we halted for lunch, our sandwiches were seen for a moment and then they mysteriously disappeared. Sources say they didn't last very long. Indeed JM commented how my sandwiches (jam) looked like they were bleeding, so it was only decent that I put them out of their misery, and ate them.

We marched on. Dale Head seemed very far away. All three of the musketeers felt drained as we descended to Dalehead Tarn and contemplated the slog up to the summit of Dale Head. It was on the steep eastern flank of Dale Head that the call of nature called to us. What do you do when you just need to go? There was only one thing for it. We each found a suitable rock to cower behind, and did our business. It can only be hoped that the fellow hill walkers we could see in the far distance didn't happen to look upwards at the crucial moment. After that refreshing interlude we continued up the fell to the summit. Dale Head has a fine cairn, but we only paused briefly as it was already three o'clock in the afternoon and we still had a long way to go.

Hindscarth and Robinson were our two final fells of the day. As we walked along Hindscarth Edge the mist dissipated and we finally had some views! We eagerly lapped up the scenery around us, it having been denied to us for most of the day. Hindscarth has good views across to the High Spy ridge, and it was with interest that we looked back along our route. We made the short circuit around to Robinson, and considered our position. Did we want to descend to High Snockrigg and cope with Buttermere Moss (which would be potentially rather uncomfortable, not to say rather soggy)? Or did we fancy the steeper descent to Hassness, following the fence as a guide? The latter route won. Steep does not describe our descent adequately. Parts were so badly eroded it was like a chute had been carved out of the soil for us to slide down. We all fell over at least once, and EJ and JM turned this into a new sport: fell sliding! It was tremendous fun, despite causing a few bruised bottoms. Needless to say, I photographed the action as evidence (just in case). Upon reaching the road, we still had about a mile of walking before we reached Buttermere village, so we set off sharply. The fast pace set was more due to urgency than to our energy levels – we were in danger of missing our tea! Despite being fleet of foot and hungry to boot, we were eagle-eyed enough to spot a slow worm slithering across the road before us. The legless lizard looked at us curiously, and then glided away over the tarmac.

After almost nine hours of walking, we crawled into Buttermere Youth Hostel. We had missed tea. It was a miserable feeling. Upon hearing of our plight and of how we had walked from Keswick to Buttermere to find no hot food waiting for us, the wonderful staff at the hostel cooked some especially for us. Our gratitude was overwhelming, and after being shooed away to stow our rucksacks in our dormitory, we returned to the mess hall. A delicious tomato soup, Cumberland sausage and mash, and chocolate fudge cake with ice cream were exactly what we needed after a long day in the mountains. During the evening – in classic youth hostel tradition – we played board games. To summarise: the first day of our two-day walking spectacular was marvellous. Could day two be even better?

Day two dawned fine and bright. After a hearty hostel breakfast we laced up our boots and set out for the great outdoors. On our way down to the lake we ventured inside St. James' Church in Buttermere to take a look at Alfred Wainwright's memorial. Looking through the window, we saw the sleepy valley and admired Haystacks, which was gently silhouetted against the sky. Just as impressive as Haystacks was the skilled craftsmanship put into creating the Shepherd's Gate, which is the ironwork gateway providing entrance to the church. The image of the shepherd tending his flock is symbolic in both religion and agriculture, whilst – in purely practical terms – the physical gate must help prevent marauding sheep from chewing the pews.

Our ascent of Red Pike began with a stroll through woodland before heading upwards to Bleaberry Tarn. The landscape surrounding the tarn felt very surreal, like a space age crater hollowed out by alien craft. What followed next can only be understood by the nickname we have since given to the particular stretch of red scree path commonly known as The Saddle. We now refer to it as 'the Death Ascent', to be spoken of in hushed and frightened tones. It began simply enough, with a little scree and a smidgeon of steepness. Then the path seemed to split in two. As both headed upwards, it didn't really matter which one we followed as both would gain us the summit ridge. Only, it did matter. It mattered quite a lot. We diligently toilet (perhaps a Freudian slip – I mean 'toiled') upwards, and entered a near vertical gully with rock at either sides. I soon found myself clinging on to rock edges with my fingertips, hauling myself upwards inch by inch. Where was the path? There was no going back, unless we chose to fling ourselves downhill and roll all the way back to the tarn. The only way was up. Heavy breathing and deep concentration. Falling was not an option. I found myself crawling up like a crab, hands grasping and feet failing to get any sort of purchase on the scree. I was scared. We were meant to be walking, not rock-climbing! I glanced down below to my companions, who were faring no better. There was only one thing for it. Desperately struggling, I launched myself up the gully and let out a bellowing grunt as I flopped onto the summit.

I had made it! Relief washed over me and cold sweat covered my body. I turned around and walked back to the edge. My friends were still down there. I began calling words of encouragement.

"You can do it! You're really close – only a few feet further!"

EJ clambered out to join me. Her face mirrored mine. Then the words you really don't want to hear came from the gully below our feet.

"I'm stuck."

I like to think it was our cheering words which propelled JM to unstick herself and join us on the ridge. In reality, it was probably our threats that we didn't want the shame of having to call for mountain rescue that forced her to creep up the scree gully towards us. In retrospect, rather than taking the path to the right we should have gone for the path on the left. This became painfully obvious when a few minutes later a couple with a dog came strolling over the edge as if they had not a care in the world. They wouldn't have looked so smug if they had chosen our path. The couple looked at us curiously as we sat limply by the cairn shovelling chocolate bars down our throats in an attempt to claw back our drained energy reserves. It was our toughest ascent yet. The three musketeers had conquered Red Pike in style!

In comparison, High Stile and High Crag were rather tame affairs, and the latter fell was our designated lunch spot of the day. Sunshine emerged from the behind the clouds and we enjoyed our first glimpse into the secluded Ennerdale valley as we traversed the ridge. From High Crag's summit cairn we could see the whole of our route down Gamlin End and across to Haystacks, and we were eager to explore Wainwright's fell. It was a steep descent off High Crag, but there is a very good zigzag path to follow, preventing further erosion of the fell. As we descended to Scarth Gap, I contemplated why Seat isn't a Wainwright, for it is just as interesting, and higher, than many of the fells Wainwright included in his two hundred and fourteen fells. Perhaps Wainwright was so overawed with nearby Haystacks that poor Seat didn't get a look in. Such is life!

Haystacks was charming. It was pretty. Purple heather and cairns and tarns are plentiful. It felt like we were paying homage to Wainwright in climbing to the summit and surveying Lakeland from this hallowed spot. But (there is always a 'but', isn't there?) there were too many people. I am sorry to say that I fell out of love with Haystacks the moment the delightful scrambles ended and I set foot on its heathery top. At least thirty contented walkers and canines were milling around, leaning on this rock, or posing for a photograph on that one. After hours of seeing only a few other souls it was quite a shock (and would be quite a shock for Wainwright too, I imagine). Sorry, Mr. Wainwright, for I'm sure Haystacks was lonely and wild when you were fellwandering over her. We paused for only a few minutes before making our way back down to Scarth Gap. It was then that we looked at the time. Originally, our plan had been to continue over Haystacks, make our way towards Dubs Quarry and on to Fleetwith Pike. However, it wasn't long into our walk that we decided such a route might be too long to comfortably fit in with the bus timetable. It was only when we returned to Scarth Gap that we realised we had just under one hour to return to the valley floor, make our way along the full length of Buttermere, and get to the village bus stop. If we missed the bus, we would be forced to either order a taxi or walk back to Keswick. The former would be expensive, and the latter unthinkable. The race was on.

We hurtled down the fell side, narrowly avoiding broken ankles on the way. Upon reaching the lake, we paused. Our bodies were tired and our legs were aching. With barely a glance at each other, in perfect unison we began to sprint along the lakeside path. Pine cones, rocks, and branches tried to trip us up but we nimbly leapt over them like a trio of gazelles. Half way along, we began to tire. With rasping breath we slowed to a laboured walk. Twenty minutes to go. Fifteen minutes. Ten. JM slowed to a halt. With a cry of "We'll stop the bus for you!" EJ and I dashed onwards to the village, eyes darting about for signs that we had made it in time. There was no bus. There were a few people milling around near the bus stop. We had made it! JM followed not far behind and we three crumbled into an ungainly pile of limbs, sweat dripping off our brows. Two minutes later, the 77 Honister Rambler bus tootled into Buttermere, and there can't have been three more grateful passengers on it that day than us. Sitting in silence, we enjoyed the journey to Keswick, thinking of what we had achieved over the past two days. It was only later that we realised the bus could have been boarded from Gatesgarth Farm, which is much closer to Scarth Gap and would have saved us from the race along the lake. Never mind, we now have a good story to tell during long winter evenings. We wolfed down portions of fish and chips in a Keswick car park and were chauffeured back home to Grasmere, regaling our housemates with tales of deathly ascents, rough lake crossings, fell sliding, uninhabitable mountains, and a frantic sprint finish. They seemed strangely unimpressed by our Herculean endeavours, merely rolling their eyes and brushing it off as Wainwright-related madness. Secretly, I'm sure they wished they could have been there, too.

After the excitement of our trip had faded into a haze of joyful memories and leg muscles had finally stopped aching, thoughts turned to my next outing into the mountains. I opted for another day of gathering odds and sods together into a multi-trip day. As such, I found myself in Kentmere again much sooner than I had anticipated, with the aim of walking the full length of the Garburn Pass, taking in Sallows and Sour Howes en route. The former fell did indeed have a sallow complexion as I followed the grassy path to the summit. Despite its sickly name, Sallows is an interesting little fell. The summit has no cairn, only a long mound which resembles a medieval barrow mound. I fully expected a Tolkien-esque barrow wight to loom up out of the mist and try to capture my soul, but there was only silence. Unsettled by the gloom, I quickly moved on. Whilst Sallows sounds poorly, Sour Howes sounds bad-tempered and grumpy. I much prefer the fell's friendlier local name of Applethwaite Common. As it happened, Sour Howes wasn't particularly welcoming that day, as it took me some time to find the summit in amongst the many humps on the fell. What is more, every time I turned around a huge hulking beast appeared. Not a barrow wight, but a herd of cows. I'm not sure who was more startled, the cows or me.

Troutbeck is an extremely pretty village which sits along the Kirkstone Pass. Therefore it feels appropriate that its namesake fell, Troutbeck Tongue, is a cute miniature mountain with valley views of Windermere which rival those from higher fells. Though secluded, there are many paths around the fell, and there is even a useless stile. I say 'useless', for it is situated in the centre of a field; its surrounding fence long gone although the signpost to Thresthwaite and stile remains. Ever

The stile without a fence. I wonder if it ever feels lonely?

the courteous walker, I made sure to climb over the stile rather than walk around it – I'm sure the nearby sheep wondered what I was doing! I would like to return to the Tongue and fully explore the nooks and crannies around it, for my quick ascent and descent (there and back again from Hagg Bridge) did not do the fell justice.

The next fell in my itinerary that day does not receive such a glowing review. Hartsop above How, like Sergeant Man, is one of the fells which for one reason or another gave me such a hard time I have no intention of ever going back. The walk started innocently enough from the red telephone box at Deepdale Bridge. I gained the ridge, which never seemed to end – it went on, and on, and on. And on some more with no real feel of any progress being made. The sun went in and the rain came out. Heavy blobs of cold wetness enveloped me and visibility was severely reduced. My boots became waterlogged and my socks saturated. The reward? A dull summit with a puny cairn. It was a slog to get up there and a slog to get back down. I was not impressed, and my overriding memory of Hartsop above How is that it is an irritating fell, and one which I was glad to have 'ticked off'. Despite my cross mood, lunch in the rain was rather refreshing. As I descended I vowed not to walk again that day, as all I wanted was to go home and curl up with a good book.

Having already summitted four fells that day, I felt it was a respectable tally. Little did I know my dad had formulated a plan that would see us park in a small lay-by by Crummock Water. He casually mentioned that the tiny hill next to us was Rannerdale Knotts, a Wainwright. You can imagine what happened next. I laced up my boots and nipped up to the summit from Hause Point. From the summit there are fantastic views of Buttermere and Crummock Water, and I would definitely recommend Rannerdale Knotts if you are looking for a late afternoon stroll. The fell is noted for having a beautiful display of bluebells in springtime. Perhaps if William Wordsworth had happened to walk in Rannerdale rather than on the shores of Ullswater, bluebells rather than daffodils would have been the focus of his most famous poem.

A trio of fells was on the agenda for the next day. I had a hankering for peace and quiet, and Grike, Crag Fell, and Lank Rigg – the three most western fells on Wainwright's list – served that purpose admirably. Starting from Kinniside Stone Circle, I strode through the plantation and onto Grike. Wainwright would be pleased to see that the 'jungle safari' he feared has not grown, as deforestation has opened out the views. The depression between Grike and Crag Fell is squishy but doesn't last long and within twenty minutes I was on the summit looking across Ennerdale Water. On the way, I chatted to two women who were walking the same route as me. They addressed me quite abruptly.

"Have you just come from that fell over there – Grike?" one asked me.
"Yes, it's got a magnificent cairn."
"See I told you it was Grike, now we've missed it and we'll have to back for it later", the first lady snapped at the second.
"We'll go to Lank Rigg first and bag Grike on the way back then", answered the second.

I faded into the landscape. How had they managed to miss Grike? To contemplate venturing all the way to Lank Rigg only to retrace your steps to summit Grike is quite an undertaking. I can't say if the ladies followed their plan, as I left before their arguing could get any worse.

Plantations are funny places. As soon as I entered the mass of dense trees which separates Crag Fell from Whoap, there was a deathly hush. Birds stopped singing, the wind ceased whistling, and I confess that I jumped at the sound of a snapped twig more than once. Forest diversity is sorely lacking, and I was joyful to be out on the open fellside once again. I hastened to the summit of Lank Rigg and immediately set about hunting for the buried treasure, which I did not find. After searching on the internet I can reveal that the two-shilling coin (which Wainwright secreted under a rock as a reward for whoever could find it) is now a twenty pence piece. That's inflation for you.

Despite Wainwright's belief that to meet another walker here to be 'outside the realms of possibility', on Lank Rigg I had a lovely meeting with a chap who was visiting all of Lakeland's trig points with his dog. We approached the trig point at roughly the same time. To my amazement, the dog ran up to the trig and jumped straight on top, performing a balancing act that would not disgrace members of a circus (apparently they later fired the dog for receiving more applause than the clowns.) I discovered that the dog was striking a pose on top of every trig point in the Lake District, which was proving to be much more fun than the evening trudge round a park. What a canine!

There are some ridge routes which produce satisfied nods and knowing glances whenever they are mentioned. The classic horseshoe round of Helvellyn by the two edges is possibly the most famous of these routes. My own ambition loitered under the surface – I too wanted to go where adventurers had gone before. Eventually I bit the bullet, caught the bus to Patterdale, and climbed up to the Hole-in-the-Wall. It was now or never. Striding Edge stretched out in front of me, a glorious shark-toothed ridge luring me in to rock-infested crags. I shunned the path to the side and marched along the arête, negotiating the tricky scramble down The Chimney at the far end before clambering up the scree path to Helvellyn's summit. I felt invincible! I danced along the summit plateau before climbing down Swirral Edge and up again to the pointy summit of

Admiring the narrow straits of Striding Edge

Catstycam – what with all of the ups and downs I felt like a jack-in-the-box. Standing at the foot of Red Tarn I looked up at Striding Edge. Whilst I had traversed it in ideal conditions, as I looked the mist drew a veil over the arête. My mood became sombre, for the edge is a dangerous place for the inexperienced. I remembered a thrilling tale my dad told me, of how in his youth he and two companions crossed the edge in thick snow with ice axes but without crampons. He recalls cutting rock steps in the ice to reach the summit of Helvellyn, before descending down the gentler western slopes. With this in my mind, I walked onwards to my next fell. Poor Birkhouse Moor could not contend with the excitement of the day, and I paused on the latter summit for the briefest of moments before heading down to Glenridding. Today had been an unforgettable day.

It will come as no surprise to anybody who has walked in the Lake District that some days will be more memorable than others. I remember my next walk – Hartsop Dodd and Caudale Moor – more for what happened after the walk than the walk itself. EJ and I had a pleasant (yet steep) ramble up from Hartsop village with beautiful views down to Brothers Water. We skirted around the cairn hoggers on Caudale Moor and descended via St. Raven's Edge (there were no ravens). After snacking at the Kirkstone Pass Inn, we boarded the 508 bus to Windermere. At least, we tried to. As our bus moved slowly down the precarious bends of the Kirkstone Pass, it stopped. A huge coach was coming the opposite way, and they met at one of the narrowest points on the road. Both buses tried reversing to no avail. Our bus crept closer and closer to the stone wall separating us from the steep sided valley. By now, cars were backed up far into the distance from both directions. Drivers began beeping their horns. The police came. The bus drivers were shouting at each other. It was an unnerving time. EJ and I had a work engagement that evening, and we were seriously contemplating getting off the bus and walking into Windermere. Eventually the police sorted out the tangle, reversing all of the cars and ordering the coach to turn around at the top of the pass as it wouldn't cope with the narrow roads on the other side. Overall, we were delayed by one and a half hours and couldn't wait to get off the bus. Angry bus drivers are a force to be reckoned with.

My favourite children's novel is *Swallows and Amazons*, by Arthur Ransome. As a child I would have done anything to jump into the books and join the characters sailing, camping and having adventures. Consequently, when JM suggested that we climb, as she phrased it, 'the Old Man and his friends', I was more than happy to join her. Coniston Old Man became Kanchenjunga in Ransome's novels, and to follow in the footsteps of the Walker children was a long-held ambition. We planned our route carefully, following the Walna Scar

Road to Goat's Water (there were no goats) before climbing Dow Crag, The Old Man of Coniston, Brim Fell, Swirl How, Great Carrs, and Grey Friar. Dow Crag provided the first delight of the day as it has a rocky summit which requires a short scramble to reach the highest point. We were alone on Dow Crag, but moving around to Coniston Old Man we joined the hoards. Children, adults, tourists, rock-climbers, and teenagers all milled around the sizeable summit cairn. We knew the Old Man was a popular fell, but we didn't realise the world and his wife would be up there on a Monday morning! Looking down upon the pony track we could see a never-ending line of walkers snaking their way up to join us, so we beat a hasty retreat to Brim Fell. Brim Fell is only a ten-minute walk away from the Old Man, and I confess that it felt like cheating to gain another summit so quickly. From that point onwards we only saw a handful of other people, and it goes to show that some walkers are only interested in climbing the famous fells, and miss out on wonderful mountain days. Following Wainwright's list means that you will explore every inch of Lakeland's mountains, and for that I am grateful.

The final three fells of our Coniston trip are all situated fairly close together. Swirl How attracted a strange insect which attacked JM's peanut butter sandwiches. We paused at the memorial to the crew of the Halifax Bomber which crashed on Great Carrs in 1944, and admired the moonscape rockiness of Grey Friar's summit. Three separate memories which moved from the funny to the contemplative, and show that every experience of the fells is unique to the walker. Our descent down the Prison Band had us wondering if there was time to conquer Wetherlam. There was not, and we cursed the bus timetables. It would not be the last time that I cursed Wetherlam's distance. As we passed by Levers Water, a man jogged by us, his long limbs loping easily through the boggy grass and stony path. I am certain that it was the almost mythical fell-runner, Joss Naylor, having an afternoon run. Another great day of fell walking, another set of memories made.

It seems to me that when I travel on buses in the Lakes, something invariably goes wrong. On the way to Patterdale to climb Place Fell, the bus driver accidentally broke off one of his wing mirrors. I don't think his superior would be very pleased. Upon alighting at Patterdale I wound my way up to the confusing mass of paths at Boredale Hause, and turned off towards Place Fell. As I got higher, rain began to fall, and the familiar torrential downpour engulfed me as I reached the trig point. I imagine the views of Ullswater would be fantastic, had I been able to see them. I beat a hasty retreat to the valley floor, but not before I detoured to the summit of Beda Fell, which is a long, grassy ridge flanked by Boredale and Martindale, two shy valleys that are home to herds of red deer. Beda Fell was my one hundredth Wainwright – a feat of which I was suitably proud. Whilst on the summit, I struck up a conversation with a man in camouflage gear who I had gained on whilst making a beeline for the cairn (I had no time to waste – I had a bus to catch). Beda Fell was his two hundred and twelfth Wainwright. I congratulated him on his achievement, having not met anybody who was so close to finishing before. He had only The Nab (which was close by) and Slight Side (which was far away) to complete his round. When asked when he planned to finish, he answered he had no plans – he just liked roaming the fells, and would get to them eventually. My own completion of the Wainwrights couldn't come soon enough, and I was elated at breaking into three digits.

CAIRNS

Many people have their own cairn ritual. Some dance around them like tribal campfires whilst others hunt around for a stone to place reverently on the top (this in itself can be quite a feat, for the likes of Hen Comb are grassy and lacking in loose and available stones). My own habit is to walk up to the cairn and place one hand on top, whilst the other triumphantly reaches for a blackcurrant and liquorice boiled sweet. It is also a matter of personal pride never to lose face and have a rest whilst I am approaching a cairn. When I reach a cairn, however, it is a different thing altogether. Then, I permit myself to slither down into an ungainly lump of walking poles, rucksacks and what used to be a human being. That is, until I attempted to recline on the extensive cairn on Seatallan. On that day I quickly shot up and hurried away after realising that the cairn had turned into a large wasps' nest, out of which many wasps were flying angrily towards me. Suddenly I had an unexpected burst of energy.

Cairns are just as interesting as mountains in their own way. They are individual. They come in many different shapes and sizes. They are symbolic. They are a monument to hard work, stamina, and dedication. What is more, they mark the summit of the mountain. Or do they? It has often been noted that Wainwright's summits are not in fact the true summit of a hill. Rosthwaite Fell comes to mind. Whilst

Bessyboot is the summit as established by Wainwright, others believe Rosthwaite Cam to hold the honour. It has also been debated whether Brund Fell or King's How is the true summit of Grange Fell. Seathwaite Fell has three cairns (best to go to all three, just in case). Sale Fell has no cairn at all. And if anybody can show me the precise summit cairn of Blea Rigg I would be eternally grateful. Its summit holds numerous small cairns and I wandered round them all before meandering across the tops and down towards Grasmere. For all readers now clamouring in your armchairs and tents that I should go and get a GPS device, I will happily admit that I am a staunch map-and-compass-and-no-new-fangled-gadgets-type-of-girl, despite being brought up in the digital age. If it was good enough for Wainwright, it's good enough for me. Of course, Wainwright often followed his nose rather than a map. Sniffing out summits would be a wonderful superpower, sniffing your way over a cliff edge rather less so.

When considering cairns, therefore, we must consider what actually counts in claiming a Wainwright. For me, the aim was to reach all of the cairns on top of each mountain (and for ones with no cairns, such as Sallows or Armboth Fell, then to get to the highest recognisable point). I do not believe that to miss the 'true' summit as decreed by the Hallowed Gods of the Ordnance Survey is to forfeit the fell, as long as the tiny black triangle marked in the *Pictorial Guides* has at least been seen, acknowledged, waved at, sworn at, embraced lovingly, or regretfully left behind when it was time to move on. As Wainwright never scaled the Howitzer on Helm Crag, neither have I felt it necessary to clamber up and dangle my legs over the edge – notwithstanding the fact that I later did this with gusto over the top of Wastwater Screes when walking between Whin Rigg and Illgill Head. It was a good job there was no wind that day.

Cairns, to simplify them, are piles of stones. They are built for a multitude of reasons – as way markers, landmarks, and memorials, to name a few. Trig points (or 'triangulation stations') have a more scientific function, and were built to be used for geographic surveys and to help measure the country. Trigs are often easier to climb onto than cairns as they are mainly built out of concrete, and can provide a great photograph if you can stand on the top waving your arms about in triumph. Some summits have both cairn and trig, which means you can take your pick as to which you feel is the spiritual summit of the mountain. Helvellyn's cairn is higher, but the trig point is in a much better location, close to the edge looking down to Red Tarn. Lank Rigg is a very remote Wainwright, tucked away and shielded by other fells and which boasts both a trig point and a sizeable cairn. Skiddaw's trig is made out of concrete, Pillar's is stone, and I grew particularly fond of one which had a plaque naming the summit of Black Fell. Trig points are also disappointing. Why, you might ask? I answer with one word: Blencathra. Old Saddleback deserves a beacon of shining glory to compliment all of its wonderful arêtes and arresting visage which you can see from the A66. And yet all it gets is a trig point which is flat and barely noticeable, and which is often used as a dog's drinking bowl. Charming. Blencathra deserves a cairn like the Thornthwaite Beacon, mighty and strong. On behalf of all fell walkers, Blencathra, I apologise. You deserve much better.

It is a minority of walkers who don't stop at a cairn even for a moment. If they don't pause at all you may have spotted a half-naked fell runner

The humble trig point – welcomed by all who roam the fells

who whips by with a grunt and a nod, barely acknowledging the mountain they have just summitted but appreciate it in their own way. The majority stop and look and enjoy. Cairns cause conversations. Conversations that often focus on the view, the route, the weather, and, of course, the cairns themselves.

Starling Dodd is a particular favourite cairn of mine, as it is twisted and hunched, being composed of spokes of metal as well as stone. We happened upon it in swirling mist and rain, and it loomed up like an alien being. Lingmell boasts a tall and narrow cairn spiralling up into the sky. Fleetwith Pike's cairn looks like a fierce guardian of Buttermere. Lank Rigg's cairn has treasure buried nearby! Alas, I failed to find it despite searching high and lo, to the great amusement of observers. Hallin Fell is a small and delicate hill, yet is in a fantastic location with sweeping views along Ullswater. Fittingly, then, the imposing obelisk on its summit can be seen for miles around.

A pile of rusty metal. No, wait, it's Starling Dodd's summit cairn

The summits of Castle Crag and Great Gable are established memorials in their own right, and commemorate those who died in the First and Second World Wars. It is long-held ambition of mine to attend the Remembrance Sunday service which is held every year on the summit of Great Gable. Other summit cairns hold much less gravitas. Some are so poor you couldn't shake a stick at them. Or rather you could, as the highest part of the fell is sometimes indicated by a stick or fence post. Hartsop Dodd, Burnbank Fell and Lord's Seat each have a thin fencepost indicating the summit. If I was the Lord, I would have chosen a much better seat. Thornthwaite Crag has a marvellous cairn – it's a shame the Romans didn't build one like it for nearby High Steet. If they can construct walls and race horses up mountains, an impressive cairn should have been no problem. Cairns can be ironic, too. The cairn on Sail does indeed sail – there was a moat around it when I was there. I splashed across to reach it. Scoat Fell has to be one of the best – its true summit is dissected by a dry stone wall. Thus, the cairn has been built on top of the wall. Pedantic, perhaps, but precise.

During my fell walking adventures, I have also been confused by cairns. During a walk around part of the Fairfield horseshoe, we were so eager to reach High Pike that as soon as we saw an impressive cairn in the distance we made a beeline towards it. As it turns out, High Bakestones has an impressive cairn but is not a Wainwright. For some equally unintelligible reason (read: I got confused and temporarily forgot how to read a map properly) I could not find the summit of Carl Side. I wandered there and back around the summit, reached Long Side and thought it was Carl Side, saw Ullock Pike and thought *that* was Long Side. I meandered back, saw the proper summit in the distance, and eventually sorted myself out. I blame the fact that I was awake until after midnight the night before, dancing whilst dressed as a witch at a famous boy wizard themed birthday party for one of my housemates.

Throughout my journey along the path of Wainwrighting, I kept a record of my progress with a photograph of me on, in, around, or beside every cairn or trig point on each summit. If nothing else, it proves to myself that I have actually walked up each and every mountain on the list. A memento which says I WAS THERE! Naturally, this leads me onto a pet hate that has developed into an almighty loathing for a certain breed of creature who roams the Lake District. These beings are to be avoided at all costs. They are the cairn hoggers. Cairn hoggers are not merely content with striding up to the summit, admiring it, maybe placing a stone on top, taking a jaunty snap with their camera, before retiring to a respectful distance so that others can have their moment. Oh no. This clan moves in for the long haul, reclining on the summit for what seems an eternity, perhaps taking a nap, maybe slowly peeling a banana, all the while making sure that they are in the most inconvenient position to allow others to photograph or enjoy the summit.

This occurred on Caudale Moor. A group of walkers who should have known better thronged the summit. After much under the breath muttering and frowning, I managed to squeeze in between their ranks for a photograph. My wrath only expired after a brie and grape sandwich was consumed at the Kirkstone Pass Inn. Similarly, in the corner of my photograph of Steeple's summit cairn is the bodiless head of a man peeping round the cairn to have a look at what I was doing. Ditto Haystacks. Poor Wainwright – Haystacks is still lovely, but far less lonely, than when you were walking. Best go early morning or late evening to have it to yourself. Scafell Pike was the worst. I'm sure that many readers will have ascended the highest point in England many more times than I have. Twice I have conquered the mountain, once in mist and once in sunshine. Both times the summit was crawling with people who made camp with deckchairs and beer barrels. I do not kid about the beer. It was being sold in pints. I left as quickly as I could. Surprisingly, much maligned Mungrisedale Common also had people on when I visited. I followed their squelchy footsteps and we exchanged a few words before squelching on our way.

As you may have guessed, I am a cairn aficionado. If you hadn't guessed, well, you haven't been paying attention. I will freely admit that cairns came to mean quite a lot to me during my fell wandering. They were a marker of progress, and I collected them up jealously, hoarding them within my memory. I backtracked many times to check that I hadn't accidentally bypassed a cairn whilst walking in fog. I recall anxiously striding up Place Fell in the mist and rain, wondering why it was taking me so long to reach the trig point. When it eventually loomed out of the fog to the side of me I gave it a hug. Cairns and trigs are stone companions, welcoming me to each fell and saying goodbye as I left. What is more, they are companions who don't talk back and remind of you of the time when you cried because the view was so beautiful (Esk Pike) or the time you made loud noises and flapped like a bird because there was nobody around and you felt the name of the fell required it (Caw Fell).

One cairn that I feel particularly emotional towards is my final cairn which I reached at the end of my journey to complete the Wainwrights. Rather unremarkable in itself, it is of an average size. But it is *my* cairn. I shall leave you to read on and discover which cairn is the one which holds a special place in my heart. The one in which I accidentally left a souvenir of a bottle top from the celebratory drink I carried in my rucksack to the summit. However much I searched, I would have had to dismantle the cairn to retrieve it (which is, of course, a thing I would never do). It will serve as a unseen memorial to my endeavours, and one that will bring me back time and again to search for it. If you find it, please post it home.

You can't fail to take a good photo of Alcock Tarn on a sunny day in spring
If you look closely, you can make out Jack's Rake slanting upwards on Pavey Ark

The glorious Grisedale valley
Squat sentinel over the valley of Buttermere

'The Squeeze' on Lingmoor Fell. Yes, there really is a path behind that large rock. Best to keep off the pies before tackling this one

A brooding Thirlmere
Sunset over the Langdale valley

Possibly the best view in the Lake District?

Good sized, detached house in desirable location with amazing views over Haweswater. Pity about the lack of roof

Winter wonderland in the Eastern Fells
Frosty Clough Head summit

Sharp Edge on Blencathra – an exercise in cautiousness

The start of my Wasdale to Ennerdale epic, and the immense bulk of Pillar

Dawn over Blencathra and all those wonderful arêtes

THE THIRD FIFTY

The Lake District is home to a wonderful array of wild animals. One of my most memorable moments happened on a misty Thursday morning in September, on my way to Angletarn Pikes. As I walked along, I heard a faint rustle to my right. A herd of ten young red deer ran in front, behind, and across my path, their coats shining rusty golden in the sun-kissed mist. It was a truly awe-inspiring sight. I had hoped to see something of the Martindale deer herd as I hiked in the area, but didn't expect to have such a close encounter so soon with the monarchs of the dales. I had an even closer encounter of the deer kind outside my home in Grasmere on a different evening, when the sound of gravel being scattered assaulted my ear. I turned quickly, and was in time to see a lithe roe deer leap over a garden gate, hurtle in front of me, through another nearby garden and onto the road and away. Deer fences are a great idea, but after seeing how high the ruminants can jump, I fear that they are primarily useless. Never mind, it's the thought that counts.

The northern top of Angletarn Pikes is the highest, but the southern top has the better view, as it looks out over the lovely Angle Tarn. Continuing my explorations, I moved onto Brock Crags (there were no badgers, again confirming that the majority of animals and birds featured in the names of fells are not present when you climb them).

The Nab and Rest Dodd followed, with The Knott and Rampsgill Head coming up behind to complete the day. I approached The Nab with caution, for I had read much about the nasty peat hags ready to trip you up and swallow you at all times. I leapt nimbly from hag to hag, pirouetting in mid-air to escape the peat hags' brown clutches and scaring away another herd of red deer who were sedately nibbling grass in the distance. Such exercise was tiring, and I was grateful when my limbs could rest from the unplanned exertion. In all honesty, though, The Nab's peat hags are not that bad, and I feel that their notorious reputation arises more from hearsay than fact. However, there are some bogs which definitely deserve to be treated with caution. I still tremble when The Pewits are mentioned, but we'll leave a discussion of their, ahem, 'merits' for a later time.

The worst aspect of The Nab is that the out-and-back route (the only officially sanctioned way onto the deer reserve) is longer than it looks. It's safe to say that I was extremely pleased to take a rest on Rest Dodd after my return journey (well, it's only polite to do as the fell says – doubly so as the pull up onto Rest Dodd is deceptively steep). As I sat, I contemplated. I had plenty of time before the last bus was due, conditions were fair, and so I decided to wander over and bag two more summits. Spontaneity (or rather opportunity) is the way of the Wainwright bagger, and The Knott and Rampsgill Head were my targets. Both were fairly close, and the fact that both were bypassed by the hoards of walkers streaming off High Street added to their attraction. After a short sojourn on their summits I descended to Hayeswater and spent a lazy half hour basking by the sunlit water before strolling down to the bus stop.

If you have been totting up my Wainwrights, you will have noticed the number that I am approaching. If not, you might be interested to know that the next fell I climbed would see me reach the halfway point of the two hundred and fourteen fells. For this milestone, I chose the smallest fell on the list, which is less than a thousand feet high: Castle Crag in Borrowdale. There is much to like about Castle Crag, my one hundred and seventh Wainwright. It has interesting slate paths constructed to and from the summit, strongly built and looking impenetrable from below, yet simple to navigate. The summit is home to a memorial commemorating the men of Borrowdale who were killed in the First

World War. Additionally, due to the history of quarrying in the area, an abundance of slate litters the route to the top, and there are slate circles (Lakeland's alternative to crop circles) made by creative visitors to the fell. An ancient hill fort and homestead possibly existed on the summit of the fell. The caves of Castle Crag also provided a summer home to an intrepid adventurer, Millican Dalton, during the early part of the twentieth century, and he chose to evacuate himself to them during the Second World War. I can't imagine living there myself though, as it would be a little too draughty for my liking. Indeed, there is much to discover on Castle Crag. It's the sort of fell that the whole family could enjoy. I began my walk in Grange, climbed Castle Crag, explored Millican Dalton's cave, and finished in Rosthwaite. It was refreshing to focus on one single fell rather than take in numerous summits on a multi-fell hike. The weather was damp and humid, which only served to increase the overpowering impression of lush vegetation and greenery that is plentiful in the Borrowdale valley. 'The Jaws of Borrowdale' is a common phrase used to describe the narrow gap between Castle Crag and Grange Fell, but 'the Jungle of Borrowdale' might be more apt. As you can tell, I am a big fan of Castle Crag.

I enjoyed my single-fell expedition, and planned another for my next outing, this time with RF for company. Of the many and varied companions who joined me on my walks, the most frequent was music. I do not mean headphones that send out a harsh and tinny noise which is enough to drive a saint to distraction, but the music that I create with my own voice: song. I frequently sang to myself whilst walking, creating a series of theme tunes for the day. (I stopped when I saw other human beings – I do not think sheep have great taste, for they never applauded me as I strode boldly along belting out tunes from *Calamity Jane*). However, it was unusual for one single song to stick in my head for a whole walk. It was stranger still for me to share a song with a friend. I will never forget my next Wainwright outing, to Lingmoor Fell with RF, and our fascination with the television jingle about the famous tinned meat product, Spam. We sang it going up, going down, and in the car on the way home. Despite our singing, the walk was a delight, with purple heather in bloom on the fell.

Beginning at the Old Dungeon Ghyll Hotel, we walked up and onto Side Pike for a terrific view of the Langdale Pikes, before following the wall to Brown How, the summit of Lingmoor Fell. On the way we came up against an opponent to Sunday lunches, ice-creams, and treacle tarts galore. It is known as 'The Squeeze'. The Squeeze is a section of path which narrows between a rock and a hard place. There was only one thing (or should that be 'thin') for it – to take off the rucksacks, suck in the stomachs, and squeeze through as best we could. We made it (just). There is another such place near Broad Stand, on Scafell, which is nicknamed 'Fat Man's Agony'. I think I'll leave that one well alone. Descending to Bleatarn House, we followed the path around the tarn before heading homewards. Short walks in the Lake District were proving to be just as interesting as longer ones, and so I followed with yet another one a week later.

You can never be sure whether the weather forecast will be accurate or not in the Lake District, for much of the area seems to have its own micro-climate. Therefore one day, expecting sunshine, I woke up to torrential rain, and ended up enjoying a drive along the Solway Coast to Maryport, Allonby and Silloth rather than be drenched on the fell tops. However, as is also usual, on the drive back the weather turned upside down and sunshine emerged. After a quick consultation with the map, I headed up to High Pike in the Caldbeck Fells. My chosen route was a quick out-and-back using the Cumbrian Way path as a guide. I very much enjoyed the grassy tramp to the summit, and do believe that these fells behind Blencathra and Skiddaw are definitely underrated. For the walker who enjoys silence, they will find it here. Funnily enough, there is a stone bench on the summit which was occupied when I arrived. I looked around, but no bus was coming to the bench to pick me up and take me back to Nether Row, so I had to walk back myself. It was on High Pike that I realised how lucky I was to be walking the Wainwrights whilst living in Grasmere. The man on the summit was also trying to complete them, although he was based in Devon. I applaud him for his dedication, and hope that he is close to finishing, if he has not done so already. That night, after experiencing the wilds of the northern fells, I experienced the daintier wilds of the 1920s at a cocktail party for one of my housemates.

The morning after the night before, my agenda consisted of a long walk covering the remainder of the High Street ridge which I had yet to conquer, unlike the Romans. I began my expedition at Haweswater,

You won't catch a bus by waiting at this bench

walking up and over the tip of The Rigg in order to begin the long, arduous climb up to Kidsty Pike (no eagles were spotted). The Roman road would then be followed, taking in High Raise, Wether Hill, Loadpot Hill, Arthur's Pike and Bonscale Pike, before descending to Howtown. Haweswater is serenely beautiful, but it is saddening to think of the village of Mardale that was lost due to the building of the reservoir. I found the ascent to Kidsty Pike to be incredibly draining, quite a killer ascent. It was worth it, though, for the cairn is on the very airy edge of the crags. I passed many Coast-to-Coasters going in the opposite direction, and my own plans for that particular long distance walk are already afoot. I began to chat with one gentleman about the view (or lack thereof) but all he was interested in was whether certain parties of Coast-to-Coasters had already gone that way before him. He seemed disgruntled when I informed him that quite a few groups had passed me on their way down to Haweswater. Such a walk is not a race, and should be enjoyed rather than rushed.

Life is not a competition. The walk to High Raise is fairly short, but as visibility was reduced to a few metres it was useful to have a compass handy to guide my path. To contrast (we do like a bit of variation), the walk from High Raise to Wether Hill is fairly long. Over two miles of unrelenting, unchanging grassiness underfoot is enough to dampen anyone's spirits. To break the monotony, I pretended to be a Roman soldier marching across the fell top, swinging my arms stiffly back and forth.

On the summit of Wether Hill I halted my marching, stood to attention and engaged in conversation with a fellow centurion (ahem, I mean hiker). This particular soldier was not attempting to walk all of the Wainwrights. Instead, his ambition was to summit all five hundred and forty one of the Birketts (fells in the Lake District which are over one thousand feet in height and recorded in Bill Birkett's *Complete Lakeland Fells*). Rather him than me. Two hundred and fourteen are enough for now (she says, whilst dreamily contemplating the Munros...). Continuing on, I passed the remains of the Lowther House (an old shooting lodge) and reached Loadpot Hill. There were no views, as the sun that crept out whilst I stood at ease on Wether Hill had decided to hide again. Coming off Loadpot Hill I walked out of the blanket of mist and the whole vista (including a spectacular Ullswater) opened up before me. It was gratifying to see the paths I would be taking winding off into the far distance. Arthur's Pike and Bonscale Pike are two fells which both boast breathtaking views of Ullswater, especially if you head north of the summits to the edge of the crag. My dad says he will never forget the sight of me standing on the edge of Bonscale Pike, surveying the landscape (he had binoculars, not superhuman sight).

I often say that the hardest sections of any walk are usually the start and the finish. It can be hard to find the beginning of a path, and equally as hard to find a way out of neatly fenced fields and country lanes back to a waiting car. The latter occurred after I had scaled Bonscale Pike, as it took me quite some time to find the descent path between Swarth Fell and White Knotts. Eventually (after wandering back and forth for an age) I found it and made my way down. What a thigh killer! It was rather steep, and at the very end of the descent near the paved path I lost concentration, my legs slipped from under me and I performed what can only be described as a bottom slide. The trouble is, you never know who is watching you when you are on the fells. I looked up shamefacedly and tried to appear nonchalant when I saw two cows in the field opposite me staring. They did not look amoosed (sorry). I quickly went on my way. This particular soldier was in need of victuals.

You never know who's watching you!

Alliterative Lakeland fell names roll off the tongue with ease. Maiden Moor, Troutbeck Tongue, and Seat Sandal all beg to be explored. Some alliterative names are even more descriptive, and I made one such the focus of my next walk: Crinkle Crags. The very word 'crinkle' suggests a mountain with rocky landscapes and exciting scrambles. Crinkle Crags did not disappoint. Ever economical with my fell walking, I combined the Crinkles with other fells in the vicinity to create a spectacular walk, and fells on my hit list today also included Pike o' Blisco, Cold Pike, and Bow Fell. The climb up to Pike o' Blisco (beginning alongside Redacre Gill) is steep and unrelenting, with a couple of tricky scrambles to warm up the muscles, especially as you get closer to the summit. Pike o' Blisco may not be as immediately recognisable as its little lump of a neighbour Pike o' Stickle, but it does have fabulous views down the Langdale valley and over the top of Lingmoor Fell. I stood next to the cairn, breathed in the clear mountain air, and promptly sat down hard. The wind was so strong that each gust forced me into a seating position, and it was quickly time to move out of the fierce wind and into a much calmer breeze down at Red Tarn.

My next stop was Cold Pike, which bears its name well. The sun was shining but it was very cold, and hats and gloves were the order of the day. As I fumbled with the wrapping around my sandwiches, I was joined by another solo woman walker. After the usual chit chat, she commented that most people bypass Cold Pike on their way to the Crinkles and don't usually detour to the summit. I mentioned Wainwright, and she gave me a knowing glance. She was in 'the club' too. I asked how many she had managed to climb, and Cold Pike turned out to be her two hundred and thirteenth fell. She was to complete the Wainwrights the next day, with Dow Crag the final summit to be bagged. I congratulated her on such a great achievement, and assured her that Dow Crag was a suitably grand finale. It heartened me that other women were walking the Wainwrights alone. Hopefully more will follow in our stead.

After this cheering show of feminine solidarity, it was time to traverse the Crinkles. I refer to Crinkle Crags in the plural as there are actually five 'crinkles', the second one (when approaching from the south) being the highest. From Cold Pike, I could rejoin the main path to the Crinkles, or take the direct route across a rather wet marsh. Naturally, I chose the latter. It may have been soggy, but it was quick. All too soon I was in amongst the clouds and meandering up and down over the rocky Crinkles, detouring here, peeping over the crags there. I enjoy scrambling and eagerly looked out for 'The Bad Step', which is a short but difficult climb up to the highest Crinkle (and if your knees won't hold up to much scrambling there is an easier bypass path to the left). It was exhilarating and I hauled myself up there like a mountain goat. As I walked along the ridge the mist swirled to and fro, giving the fell an enigmatic and mysterious cloak. Crinkle Crags is (or should that be 'are'?) without a doubt one of my favourite fells. I was quite sad to head down towards the Three Tarns.

At Three Tarns, I was presented with a quandary. I had one and half hours before the last bus would take me from Langdale to Ambleside, yet I wanted to continue on to Bowfell. I gave myself an ultimatum: if I wasn't on Bow Fell's summit in half an hour I would turn back and head for the bus. I pressed on, hiking through the scree and rocks and boulders littering the lunar landscape of the mighty fell, reaching it in twenty five minutes, and boy, was it worth it! Bow Fell also claims a place as one of my favourite fells. I explored the summit, gazed at the Bowfell Buttress and stood at the top of the Great Slab, which is an enormous wedge of tilting rock. I did not mind that my view of the Scafell massif was hidden by cloud, as I was quite content with Bow Fell's undeniable charms. However, time was pressing and I reluctantly peeled my boots away from the summit and descended down The Band, increasing to a steady trot to reach the bus stop in time. I had ten minutes to spare, and snoozed all the way home. Today would definitely be a hard day to beat. I wondered what my next walk would have in store for me!

I did not expect my next walk to be as exciting or as memorable as Crinkle Crags and Bow Fell. I was completely and utterly wrong, as the walk involved the three musketeers reuniting for the day to cross the backbone of Wainwright's *Central Fells*. It was tiring. It was exhilarating. It was boggy. Most of all, it was one that we will never forget. We walked from Rakefoot (near Castlerigg) to Stonethwaite in Borrowdale, taking in six Wainwrights on the way: Walla Crag, Bleaberry Fell, High Seat, High Tove, Armboth Fell, and Ullscarf (the latter five fells were the ones I added to my tally, having climbed Walla Crag previously). Bleaberry Fell has a very endearing name which brings to mind summer days and fruit pies, although I'm not entirely sure what a bleaberry is. It ain't no blueberry or bilberry, that's for sure. Today's route wasn't a walk in the park, either. The whole walk can be described accurately in one word, and that word is 'bog'. After we left the summit of Bleaberry Fell, the path became a peaty morass. Our mood remained upbeat, despite knowing that we were soon to encounter some of the worst bogs in the Lake District after a period of heavy rain. We lingered a while on High Seat and contemplated the view down the ridge. The cairn across the wall from the trig point on High Seat is called 'Man' and a debate was had as to why it was not called 'Woman'. In the spirit of exploration and discovery we renamed it in honour of the fairer sex.

Sometimes strange things are encountered on the fells. Huge creatures with deformed backs (hikers with rucksacks), threatening woolly mammoths (Herdwick sheep), and Pterodactyls circle the skies (crows on the lookout). However, that day we found some truly unusual material. JM noticed them first. Creamy, translucent blobs of a jelly-like substance appeared every now and then on the path. Martian goo? Solidified frog spawn? It was very puzzling. It appears that this phenomenon is known as 'star jelly', and scientists are not fully certain of where it comes from. Suggestions have been made that it falls from the skies after a meteorite shower, and others have said that it is a type of slime mould. Whatever it is, it was fascinating to look at, and it felt very alien to the landscape. Extra-terrestrial considerations aside, it was now time to face The Pewits.

Scraggy grass turned to black bog quickly, and we knew we had reached The Pewits. It is a section of the central ridge which is the boggiest, wettest and stickiest quagmire in the whole of Lakeland. We needed to wade our way through The Pewits to reach High Tove. We jumped, we squelched, we leaped, we slithered. Adjectives are not adequate to the task of describing The Pewits. At one particularly nasty section there was a makeshift bridge consisting of a couple of fence poles. Stepping on them was precarious as the far end disappeared into the blackness. There was only one thing for it. En masse we floundered into the bog, and promptly sank to our knees. We twisted, turned, heaved and inched forward through the swamp, powered only by desperate thought. It was an anxious time. EJ emerged first, followed by myself, and then JM. Our legs made sucking noises as they exited the bog, and we clawed our way onto dry land (I say dry land, but it was more of a damp grassy hillock). The Pewits had drained us of our energy, and we temporarily made camp on High Tove. We were mightily pleased that we weren't making a return journey that way.

Armboth Fell did not do much to raise our tired spirits. It is a fell hated by many, with good reason. Perhaps on a bright day it may be different, with sunshine glinting off the purple heather and the domed summit rock a pleasant place to sunbathe. However, it was not enjoyable the day we were there. There was swampy ground, tough heather and long grass to plod through before having to wander around all of the likely-looking rocks to determine which one was the summit. I'm sure Wainwright included Armboth Fell for a reason, but I have yet to discover what that reason is. It is also a surprisingly long way to Ullscarf from Armboth Fell. We were tiring, and the three miles in between the two felt more like ten. Blea Tarn is very pretty, but we were in no mood to appreciate it. Step by wicked step we passed Middle Crag, Shivery Knott, and Standing Crag before following the line of broken fence posts to Ullscarf. Glorious Ullscarf! I could have kissed the damp grass on your summit when we eventually flopped down next to the cairn for a chocolate stop. Apart from the cairn, the summit is fairly featureless, and I could not help but think that such a central fell might have a slightly better view. Poor Ullscarf. Despite your exciting name (you sound like a hardy Viking warrior) you are a bit feeble.

Our descent route from Ullscarf was to follow the broken fence to Greenup Edge and take the path down alongside Greenup Gill. Now might be a good point to mention that we had failed to accurately calculate how long our central ridge walk would take. Suffice to say that when we approached Blea Tarn we should have been unlacing our boots down in Stonethwaite, therefore when we sat down on the summit of Ullscarf we were a couple of hours overdue. When we finally reached Stonethwaite we were four hours late and the light was fading. It was not my best moment. I hereby offer my heartfelt apologies to mum and dad, who dutifully waited those extra four hours in a spot without any mobile phone signal and were probably wondering if the pesky Pewits had sucked us in, and for us to be found centuries later, like the poor Tollund Man. To their credit, my dad has since said that he knew we would appear eventually as he had confidence in our abilities; it was just a matter of when, not where.

Whinlatter is the location of England's only mountain forest, and I made it the focus of my next walk. RF and I had a pleasant amble under the leafy canopy of the forest before emerging onto the fellside. A steep but short section took us onto the ridge, and we followed the path to the summit of Whinlatter (called Brown How). After we descended back into the trees, we began to follow the adventure play trail, and couldn't resist having a climb on the cargo net and playing with the Archimedean screw. For a number of years my personal motto has been 'you don't stop playing when you grow old, you grow old because you stop playing', and I am still a child at heart! It was on this walk that I also lost a faithful companion who had accompanied me on many of my Wainwright walks to this point. Some love them and some loathe them, but I had become fond of my walking pole. I didn't use it much, but I loved the thought of it, and it reminded me of the day I went up Knott Rigg and more experienced walkers than me (at the time) strode by with poles whilst I crouched in the wind. Call me materialistic if you will, but with my pole I felt like a 'proper' walker! Despite loving my pole (which was actually my dad's, he having given it to me as I would use it more) I walked all the way up to the summit of Whinlatter, back down, and was walking around Keswick before I realised I was missing something. Drat. Double drat. I had left my beloved pole in the toilets at the visitor centre at Whinlatter. I didn't want to have to go back for it and consoled myself with the thought that material possessions are, after all, immaterial. It is the memories that are irreplaceable. I promptly bough two more in a Keswick shop. After all, I never was one to stand on ceremony.

One of the pleasures of being a solo walker is the chance to alter and amend routes at will, whether by necessity or by design. My next walk was a combination of both. I set off from the Old Dungeon Ghyll Hotel along Mickleden, intending to scale the highest mountain in England, Scafell Pike. As I followed the Rossett Gill path the sun became scorching (this was the end of September, mind you). I considered my options. They were: climb Scafell Pike in the sweltering heat, possibly become dehydrated and not fit for work the next day, or change my route. I selected the latter option. Scafell Pike would wait for another time. Instead of the tallest peak in England I opted for three lesser, but no less impressive, mountains. They were Rossett Pike, Esk Pike, and Allen Crags. Rossett Pike's summit was a haven from the stream of walkers flowing up the path, despite it being only a short hop away. I then made my way up to Esk Pike via Angle Tarn and Ore Gap. Angle

Tarn is extremely pretty and in a dramatic location, whilst the walk to Ore Gap, whilst strenuous, was not too steep. Sublime is how I shall describe Esk Pike. The summit is rocky, much like the mini moonscape on neighbouring Bow Fell, and I devoured lunch with a magnificent view of the Scafell group. Esk Pike is (and it takes quite a lot of courage for me to admit this) the only summit on which I actually shed a few tears in awe of the spectacular beauty of my surroundings, and for that reason alone I will always remember it. I felt so lucky to have the freedom to walk in the high fells that it really took my breath away. Feeling thoroughly content and at peace with the world, I made my way down to Esk Hause, reverently picking my way down the stony path. A quick glance at my watch, a short perusal of the map, and I nipped up to the summit of Allen Crags. I spent quite some time on the boulder-strewn summit, exploring, taking photographs, and generally musing about life. It was with great reluctance that I descended to Angle Tarn and retraced my steps to Old Dungeon Ghyll. An absolutely brilliant day of walking in the September sunshine.

I am sure that other hikers will agree with me when I say that fells have distinct personalities. Some are proud, some are gentle, some are pensive, and others are cheerful. October came too swiftly for my liking, and with shorter days came the need for shorter walks. It is this that led me to suggest to JM that we take a look at two jolly little fells, Black Fell and Holme Fell, near Skelwith Bridge. These two modest peaks are separated by the A593 road, and give the impressions of often overlooked small relations to the main family group of Coniston fells to the south west. However, they are not to be bypassed in favour of the higher mountains. The summit of Black Fell has lovely views across to Tarn Hows, and Holme Fell is a delightful maze of twisting paths. On the latter, we lunched on Ivy Crag and were treated to a huge rainbow. All in all, these two jolly little fells had produced a smashing walk, to descend into the vocabulary of a *Famous Five* book. We were also treated to the sight of a man fell walking in a kilt. All I can say is that it must have been a little breezy for him.

Hiawatha was a famous Native American chieftain. Pikeawassa was not. Pikeawassa is the summit name of Steel Knotts, which I climbed from Martindale's old church, getting entangled in bracken on the way up. Thankfully, the summit ridge is grassy with rocks (no more tickly bracken) and I perched on the highest point before being blown back down the path by ferociously strong winds to the car. Have it your way, nature. I can take a hint as well as anyone! We drove round to a different section of the Lake District, and I began anew with a sick fell. Poor Barf. You are such a pretty fell but have such an ugly name. The climb up alongside Beckstones Gill must be one of the prettiest tree-clad ascents out of all the Wainwrights, with dappled sunlight dancing through the trees and the refreshing sound of water trickling downhill. I saluted the Bishop on my way. The Bishop of Barf is a large stone, painted white, and is clearly visible from the A66 when driving towards Cockermouth. Legend tells that it marks the precise spot where the Bishop of Derry fell from his horse after claiming he could successfully ride up the steep nose of the fell to the summit. Predictably, he did not succeed, and both the Bishop and his horse died after tumbling down the mountain.

With this sobering thought (more sober, perhaps, than the aforementioned Bishop) I continued my walk, taking in Lord's Seat, Broom Fell, and Graystones. The walking was easy, and I saw only one other person and a kestrel hovering for prey. The kestrel, that is, not the person. The descent to Scawgill Bridge must be one of the steepest in the whole of Lakeland, and I was very glad to be going downhill, rather than up. Ever the glutton for punishment, I was still not content with my day, and finished off with a saunter up and along the Knott Rigg and Ard Crags ridge. Having summitted Knott Rigg previously, I thought I knew what to expect from the continuation of the ridge, but I was wrong. I anticipated the ridge to be wholly lush, grassy and green, but it turned out to be schizophrenic. Past Knott Rigg, the green and pleasant land ends and Ard Crags becomes wild, heathery and rocky like the desolate moorland of the North York Moors. It is a fascinating ridge and demands further exploration. However, my Wainwright appetite was satiated for the day, and after negotiating a herd of angry-looking cows, it was time to head home.

My next walk was considerably shorter than the last, but by no means less dramatic. Of all the bodies of water in the Lake District, one which seems perpetually moody is Thirlmere. Dark and brooding, it lies like a leviathan sucking in sunlight from the surrounding mountains. Its presence has an effect on the nearby fells, and my walk to the summit of Raven Crag equalled the sullenness of the reservoir. My legs dragged upwards and twigs clawed at my hair. Humid air lingered in amongst the branches and there was a hush in the forest. On the final push to the summit I encountered huge fallen trees, traps for the unwary. Eyes darting about, I moved through the thickets to emerge victorious at the cairn, yet no birdsong greeted my arrival nor did any human voice bid me welcome. I strode to the edge of the cliff to view the reservoir stretching away into the distance and watched the waves ripple along the surface. We've all heard of the popular myth that there is a creature in Lake Windermere, but on that day I wouldn't have been at all surprised to see a shadowy form glide under the surface of Thirlmere. Raven Crag was a surprising fell, as no other Wainwright made me feel quite so alone. Fells definitely do have personalities, and Raven Crag left me quite unsettled. I definitely needed to plan a more cheerful walk for next time!

Next time soon came around, and I headed for the sunny heights of the fells in North West Cumbria. Today was going to be one of those serendipitous days in which I ditched my plans halfway through, threw caution to the winds and had a downright great walk. Such are the days that we hikers long for! I began in the village of Braithwaite and ended in the village of Buttermere, scaling the summits of Barrow, Outerside, Sail, Crag Hill (Eel Crag), Grasmoor, Wandope and Whiteless Pike along the way. Barrow is a quick hop, skip and a jump from Braithwaite, and it was satisfying to reach the summit so quickly, with extensive views (particularly good of Skiddaw) that would reward a much longer walk than that needed to scale Barrow. Whilst eagerly drinking in the view, I had a natter with an elderly gentlemen who had walked all of the Wainwrights, lived in Cockermouth, and often caught the bus and walked where his feet led him. He wished me luck in my endeavours, and I wished to still enjoy walking in the Lakes at his age.

Outerside was next, and at the summit I added further 'Outer' layers of clothing to my body (did you see what I did there?), as the wind had picked up and the weather was pretty cold. I sailed on to Sail, and endured the walk up to the summit with patience. A brand new winding zigzag path had been created which I thought was a complete eyesore. I sincerely hope that it blends in with time and does help to stop erosion of the fell. Nevertheless Sail is a very whimsical fell, with the cairn stood in the centre of a pool of water. A coracle would have been useful to reach it, but I leaped across to the island cairn instead. The things we do for our Wainwrights, eh! The scramble up The Scar to the summit of Crag Hill (also known as Eel Crag) was invigorating, and I reached the trig point with a huge grin on my face. The whole of the Lake District spread out before me in every direction, and I was in love with life. It was here that I ditched my original plan, which was to climb back down The Scar and descend over Scar Crags and Causey Pike. However, I could not waste such good weather and after a quick check of the bus timetable I made a beeline for Grasmoor.

Grasmoor is a hulking beast, dominating views in the Loweswater area and drawing all eyes ever upwards. Invigorated by life, I explored the summit plateau and planned my descent. Lunch was had in the main cross-shelter, where inquisitive sheep nosed around hopefully. They weren't having any of my sandwiches, though. From Grasmere to Grasmoor I had come, and onto Wandope I went (as you can tell, I am a fan of alliteration). Wandope is an unassuming fell, but is one of the few places where you can see the Knott Rigg – Ard Crags summit ridge in great detail from above.

As I made my way between Wandope and Whiteless Edge, two people approached me, commenting that they could see I had a map, and that they had come up without one! They wanted to know the names of each and every mountain that could be seen in the distance and where they were on my map. As I am not a walking Ordnance Survey vending machine, I limited my description to the fells immediately around us. After I had patiently named the fells they asked me to suggest a "nice round trip to take us from where we are in a circle and back into Buttermere." As they disregarded any attempt to hint that they were better off going back the way that they had come, I tentatively suggested they ascend the summit of Grasmoor and follow the ridge down Lad Hows (visibility was excellent, and the path could clearly be seen from where we were standing). This was rejected as being too long, and I explained that as any other circular walk would be equally, if not longer, than that to Grasmoor and back, perhaps they should consider continuing onto Wandope and making their way down again, especially as they had no map. The couple debated between themselves and formed a plan whereby "we'll walk as far as we can and then come back." Shaking my head in disbelief I made my goodbyes and walked on. I hope that they enjoyed their walk, but cannot stress how – even on the clearest of days – it is necessary to bring a map along for the journey. These were adults, too! Sometimes I worry not for the next generation, but for the current one.

Leaving the pair to their own devices and hoping that they acted sensibly and headed back down the ridge to explore villages and tearooms rather than mountains and summits, I marched onto Whiteless Edge and paused on Whiteless Pike. The ridge is narrow and rocky with glorious views, and is a last chance to enjoy the excitement of the high Lakeland fells before descending to Buttermere village. Spontaneous walks are a marvellous thing, and it was a contented walker who snoozed on the buses back to Grasmere at the end of the day.

Having altered my plans mid-walk during my Braithwaite to Buttermere epic, I was eager to climb the abandoned fells of Causey Pike and Scar Crags. Consequently, a windy October morning saw me lace up my boots, take to the hills, and tackle the aforementioned twosome. Causey Pike is one of those fells which is recognisable from miles around, with a knobbly little lump on top and a bumpy ridge like a miniature Crinkle Crags. It did not take long to reach the summit from Braithwaite, and I surveyed my Lakeland kingdom proudly. Strong blustery bursts tried to knock me off my feet as I walked the ridge between Causey Pike and Scar Crags, and I and other walkers lost our footing on several occasions. It was as if Scar Crags didn't want me to claim its summit, so fiercely did the wind try to send me tumbling down the crags below. Scar Crags is one of those fells which has a fantastic name, conjuring up ferocious beasts and brutal ascents. Yet the fell is a quiet, tame animal (at least when the winds die down), and I'm sure many people climb it by accident rather than by design, on the way to grander mountains or as part of the Coledale Horseshoe. It was hugely satisfying to bag the two fells (despite my aversion to the term 'bagging') and I knew it wouldn't be long before I completed book number six of Wainwright's *Pictorial Guides.*

If you ask any number of hikers to name the most iconic mountains in the Lake District, I'm sure that the answers will vary quite substantially. However, I am sure that one particular name will crop up more times than others. Great Gable. Presiding at the head of Wasdale, Great Gable stands proudly, its domed top visible for miles around. I had long desired to climb its hallowed flanks. Finally, I got my opportunity. My selected route began from the Honister Pass (some people say this is cheating, but as I had to rely on the local bus service I feel justified in approaching Great Gable from the Honister side). Mountains on the agenda today were Grey Knotts, Brandreth, Green Gable, Great Gable, Base Brown, and Fleetwith Pike. A steep pitched path led me to the summit of Grey Knotts, where I had my first glimpse of the main target of the day. Great Gable was covered in cloud. Never mind. Brandreth followed swiftly after, and my footsteps led me on to Green Gable. I am ashamed to say that I did not give these fells the attention that they deserve, as I was more focused on reaching Great Gable than I was on the fells crossed along the way. I did, however, halt on Green Gable. Great Gable's white cap had disappeared and I gazed upwards, mesmerised. The orange scree path down and up Windy Gap looked dangerously inviting, and the rocky scramble to the summit called out to me. I couldn't wait any longer, and like a steam train I hurtled down Windy Gap and began the push to the summit. To continue the metaphor, upon arrival I disembarked at the summit platform (cairn), put down my luggage (rucksack), and surveyed my destination (Great Gable). I can easily sum up this mountain in one word which I am sure many will agree with: magnificent.

Great Gable was my one hundred and fiftieth Wainwright, and it truly is a fell that dreams are made of. Legends are formed around Great Gable. Features such as the Napes Needle, Sphinx Rock, and the Westmorland Cairn send shivers of excitement down my spine, and I know that I will definitely climb Great Gable many more times in my life. It is one of my ambitions to attend the yearly Remembrance Sunday memorial service which is held on top of Great Gable each year and must be an extremely moving occasion. After I had drunk my fill of Great Gable and its panoramic views, I dragged my feet away in the direction of Windy Gap and my next summit, Base Brown, which could not compete with its predecessor. However, Base Brown does have a large cairn and first-rate views of Gillercomb and Seathwaite which compensate for the major shortcoming of not being Great

Gable. As for me, it was onto Fleetwith Pike with fleeting footsteps. I skirted around Gillercomb Head, joined Moses Trod, bypassed Brandreth and Grey Knotts, made my way across to the Drum House and followed the path to Black Star and beyond to the summit of Fleetwith Pike. The summit cairn of Fleetwith Pike acts as a squat little sentinel to the fell, guarding the way down to Buttermere and Crummock Water. I spent quite some time here, gazing at the view and resting my weary legs. All too soon I climbed down Fleetwith Edge and caught the bus back home. Fleetwith Edge is a fantastic craggy descent route, keeping my interest until the very end. If Fleetwith Pike happened to have been my final Wainwright, to climb it by Fleetwith Edge would make a fitting culmination of the 214 fells, and the view of the lakes below a just reward. At this point I hadn't really considered what my final Wainwright would be, and simply hiked as the opportunities presented themselves.

VIEWS

'Views' is an ambiguous word. Does it refer to rolling vistas, far-off horizons, and mesmerising landscapes? Or are opinions, thoughts and judgements the principal meaning of the word?

One particular question causes me to form my own views of the Lakeland fells, whilst contemplating their location, attributes, and, importantly, the view from the summits. 'What is this question?' I hear you ask.

"Which is your favourite fell?"

The above question is the most difficult one of all to answer. Yet to walk the Wainwrights is to inevitably put the Lake District fells in direct competition with one another, whether for attention, for favouritism, for good opinions or stand-out memories. I have always been reluctant to do so, believing that all of the fells, with the exception of a very few (I'm looking at you, Hartsop Above How), have a special 'something' to share with the discerning hiker. Nevertheless, I am constantly asked this question. When Wainwright finished writing and illustrating his seventh *Pictorial Guide*, in his notes of conclusion he selected his favourite six mountains, six summits, and six ridge walks. Every fell walker will have their own opinion with regards to which fells should have the honour of inclusion, but will likewise believe that as each person's journey towards completing the Wainwrights is very personal, so too will be their choice of the 'best fells'. I have thought long and hard about a suitable response to the question regarding my favourite fell, and, in answer, have produced my very own Lakeland Awards Ceremony, where the fells are the stars of the show. I chose categories which made me pause and contemplate every single Wainwright – an undertaking which was in itself pleasurable as I pondered all two hundred and fourteen fells, including some and rejecting others. I wonder if you agree with my choices?

Prettiest fell name
1. Maiden Moor
2. Glaramara
3. Catbells

Ugliest fell name
1. Barf
2. Grike
3. Birks

Most exciting mountain
1. Yewbarrow
2. Crinkle Crags
3. Great Gable

Most irritating mountain
1. Hartsop Above How
2. Wetherlam
3. Scafell Pike

Most underrated mountain
1. Lank Rigg
2. Mungrisedale Common
3. Low Fell

Most interesting summit
1. Castle Crag
2. High Street
3. Helm Crag

Most beautiful valley encountered
1. Longsleddale
2. Wasdale
3. Far Easedale

And my answer to the question which prompted these ponderings? A few come very close, although I wouldn't want to choose between them. Silver How, Yewbarrow, and Castle Crag all spring to mind, but there isn't an outright frontrunner. My favourite fell changes constantly, depending on the mood I'm in, and whether I favour a dramatic ridge walk, a gentle saunter or simply a spectacular view which holds many special memories. As fell walkers, we retain the right to backtrack, change our minds, and add new favourites to the list each time we head out into the countryside.

Indeed, some aspects of fell-walking change constantly. Weather reports should always be treated with caution, and fantastic views alter with every single step taken. However, after much trial and error, certain things that I do stay the same, time after time. These are the clothes that I wear, and the food that I eat. Although I am certainly no expert, I will share with you a few thoughts (or rather, 'views') about such matters which I have formulated whilst walking the Wainwrights.

I have read many reviews, articles and books about what to eat when out in the mountains. "Energy foods!" the advertisements cry. "Special hill walking snacks which could prevent the onset of hypothermia!" I cast a suspicious glance at such foodstuffs. When on the hills, all I desire is filling, familiar, and comforting food. Therefore, my basic lunchbox usually contains the following items: a cheese sandwich (because everyone loves cheese, don't they?), a jam sandwich (great for that last burst of energy towards the end of the day), crisps (it has to be salt and vinegar flavour), raisins (sweet and juicy), and miscellaneous flapjacks and cereal bars (satisfying). I experimented with paste sandwiches, but more often than not found them squished to a pulp next to my fleece in the bottom of my rucksack. For some reason, jam sandwiches seem to hold their shape (but need to be wrapped up in many layers to prevent them bleeding jam everywhere). Water is a wonderful drink to carry and you should aim to carry a few litres, but a hot drink in a flask can warm you up quicker than jogging on the spot will.

Depending on the weather conditions, I try to stay away from chocolate (melts in summer and becomes solid enough to break a tooth during the colder months). I do however, keep a couple of well-known chocolate-covered, caramel nougat bars branded with the name of a distant red planet in my emergency rations, as they are fantastic for perking you up if feeling low (my personal record is eating three in one day). I also stash an undisclosed quantity of boiled sweets in various pockets, which can sustain me until my next planned fuel stop. Blackcurrant and liquorice is my preferred flavour, but I was once forced to take chocolate limes out of necessity. Never again. I have one friend who swears by malt loaf and homemade fruitcake, and another who brings enough packets of jelly babies to withstand a month-long siege. Trial and error is the only way to determine what you enjoy eating when out on the fells, and whether pies, pasties or paninis are your thing, just make sure you take enough so you don't go hungry!

Clothing and rucksack paraphernalia present a different quandary, but a quandary nonetheless. You want to wear garments which will protect you from the elements, look halfway decent, and last (hopefully) for more than a few years before they wear out. You quite like the bright blues, reds and yellows that greet your eyes in any outdoor shop. Yet at the same time you don't want to look like someone who spends more time in walking shops than actually out walking. The solution is simple. Buy the clothing that you want, head out to the Pewits (some of the worst bog in central Lakeland) on a rainy day, and return home so black and grimy that you cannot wash the mud out and others will see you as a hardened fell walker.

Realistically though, you should aim to wear clothes that make you feel comfortable, warm, and waterproof. This is usually found in layering a mixture of short-sleeved t-shirts, fleeces, waterproof coats, long-sleeved tops, and even straying into the mysterious realms of wicking base layers and soft shells. Layers mean that when it's hot you can take them off, and when it's cold you can put them on. Hats and gloves are a must. Even in the height of summer I keep them stored in my rucksack. It may be hot in the valleys, but it can be chilly up on the tops. Gaiters are a tricky one. For years I ignored them as superfluous clothing but am a recent convert. No longer do I come back with walking trousers plastered high with mud and needing a thorough scrub. Water doesn't trickle into my socks from the top of my boots in a flash rainstorm. They may look funny, but I now look knowingly at fellow walkers who wear them. The dry feet club is a good club to be in.

Most importantly, be sensible with your clothes. If you are walking a very short, low level walk in the middle of a dry August in a popular area, it is perfectly alright to leave your coat behind, rather than cursing its presence as you stuff it into your rucksack. I've lost count of the times I've walked around Ambleside and seen whole families trussed up as though they were climbing Mount Everest, when in reality it's mid-July and they've only been to the head of Lake Windermere. In a not-unrelated note, please avoid jeans and high heels when walking up a fell. Jeans won't dry if you get them wet and you will become cold very quickly, and heels are crying out for a broken ankle. As much as we respect and admire the mountain rescue teams, we don't really want to meet them out on the fells when we could easily have prevented a casualty by using common sense. I had to look twice when I saw the rather glamorous girl teetering in high heels on Scafell Pike, and glanced askance at my water bottle. What had I been drinking?

Every walker I know has their personal favourite item of clothing, and it's not always the most fashionable. I myself am guilty of harbouring an irrational love of a pair of yellow, woollen, knee-length walking socks (formerly my mum's skiing socks) from the 1970s. Yes, they have holes. Yes, they are incredibly heavy when wet. However, it takes an extraordinarily long time for them to get wet because they are so thick. It's only recently that I've taken the plunge and bought fancy new hiking socks with waterproof this and breathable that, as my faithful yellow companions have now walked one step too far. It's not for any reason that I wanted to subtitle this book 'Yellow Sock Walker'.

Fundamental to the act of walking up and down mountains in the Lake District (and anywhere else in the world for that matter) is what you put on your feet. Your walking boots are the best friend that you will have on a mountain. Chosen well, they will offer support, prevent blisters, and protect your feet. When, after years of hard use, they are forced to retire, you will look upon their passing with regret (and most likely, will never throw them away). Leather or softer materials will both do the job well. Consider the terrain you will encounter, the time of year, and the likely weather. Take your time, wear them at home, and don't be afraid to take them back to the shop if they start to rub after wearing them for a few days at home and up and down the stairs. Try to avoid being swayed by price, as quality can be found in some of the cheaper items, if you look long enough. Knowledgeable employees are the lifeblood of the outdoors shop, and good ones will understand if you say that something is wrong, even if you can't pinpoint what that 'something' is.

Choosing the right rucksack is as important as choosing the right boots. It should be comfortable, have well-fitting shoulder straps, be the correct size for your trip, have the right amount of pockets for your needs, and ideally be waterproof (as much as any rucksack can be). I approach the contents of my rucksack with similar experimentation. I began by having an I-must-carry-everything-that-I-might-possibly-need-for-any-eventuality mindset, but soon realised that this wasn't practical (it was also very heavy). However, there are some essentials that you must not do without. A map and a compass, with the usual old adage that it's not good enough to purely own them, you must know how to use them. Learn the essentials of map-reading from books or the internet, or better still, get a friend to teach you. You don't want to be stuck in thick fog on an expansive plateau and not know how, or where, to get down. A small first aid kit is highly useful, and a whistle necessary for the (hopefully never encountered) occasion where you need to signal for help (six long blasts on the whistle, pause for one minute, and repeat). Consider having a thermal blanket or survival bag tucked away somewhere for use too. The phrase 'just in case' is a useful one in this instance. Spare layers of clothing, hat and gloves, sun cream and sunglasses for sunny days, a torch in case you come home in the dark (with working batteries!), food and drink, and emergency rations all find their way into my rucksack.

A fully charged mobile phone (although I admit one thing I love about mountain tops and remote valleys is the lessening chance of having mobile phone reception) and a camera for the budding photographers among us (or those who want to prove that we were there). A walking pole is useful for checking the depth of suspicious looking boggy patches, fending off wolves and bears, and providing aid when crossing deep streams. I also take a couple of spare plastic bags. They don't weigh much, but can be used as makeshift seats on damp ground, to wrap up leaking bottles, collect rubbish, and as liners if your rucksack liner splits. Other objects – such as binoculars, guide books, and kitchen sinks are individual to every walker. Only remember the cardinal rule: if you put it in the rucksack, you are the one who carries it.

THE FOURTH FIFTY

The only golden eagle in England makes the Lake District his home. I was hopeful that I might glimpse such a majestic creature whilst climbing up Eagle Crag with JM, but the eagle kept to his usual haunts around Haweswater that day. Alas, the many minutes spent straining our eyes against small dark specks in the sky were in vain. We saw a good many crows, though, and a heron. Two herons, in fact. However, if I were an eagle, or any other bird for that matter, I would have stayed away on the day we ascended Eagle Crag. Rain poured from the sky – whole kettles of it – which saw us scurrying for cover amongst the rocks and heather. There wasn't any. Cover, that is. There was plenty of rocks and heather. The gully was an exciting addition to the ascent, and, if the weather were finer, Georgian dresses would have been more appropriate to wander back and forth along the terraces than hiking gear. Wainwright sure knew how to plan a good walk. The summit has a sizeable rock plateau where we enjoyed making eagle impressions. It's a good job there were no eagles around to witness our dismal attempts to be the king of the skies. We continued along the ridge and reached Sergeant's Crag. Typically, there were no sergeants either. Come on, Lakeland fells – try to give us what you promise us in your names!

On the final approach to Sergeant's Crag, I spotted a suspicious looking watery hole and sidestepped it. I didn't mention it to JM as it was fairly large and I thought she couldn't possibly miss it. She did. A piercing squeak sounded behind me, I whipped around and JM was standing up to her knees in the boggy hole. Ever resourceful, she climbed out, zipped off the bottom section of her trousers (they were the fancy kind which can turn into shorts if the weather is unexpectedly sunny, or if you fall into a hole) and we were on our way. Sergeant's Crag was the site for our luncheon, which we ate ravenously. We then had a choice (life is full of these pesky things). Return the way we had come, or descend down the eastern face of Sergeant's Crag, walk through the grassy terrain, cross Greenup Gill and follow the gill path back to Stonethwaite. Naturally, we two eager explorers chose the latter option, and were rewarded with a fun experience of what we called 'proper wild walking' (meaning no path). Our feet got, if possible, even soggier, but it was two happy walkers who caught the bus at Rosthwaite later that day.

Some legendary sightings in the Lake District are even rarer than managing to spot the elusive golden eagle. On one Midsummer's Day in the eighteenth century, Souther Fell was the focus of a much more extraordinary, perhaps even supernatural, event. A long line of soldiers and cavalry were seen marching across the fell for many hours, vanishing into nothingness as soon as they left the ridge. Mysteriously, there was no evidence of the soldiers the next day, as the ground is soft but no foot imprints could be found. Reliable (and sober!) witnesses swore that the troops were real, and they have, apparently, been seen a few times since. I remained hopeful as I walked along the summit ridge, but there was no rhythmic boot marching to be seen or heard anywhere, and no flash of tartan plaid appeared in the corner of my eye (some believe the soldiers to have been Bonnie Prince Charlie's troops). Perhaps I need to go back on a Midsummer's Day, just in case. Then again, even if a spectral army had danced by doing the conga I probably wouldn't have noticed as I stopped and stared, awestruck at my first proper view of the mighty Sharp Edge.

Sharp Edge. Whisper it in hushed tones. It must be one of the most exhilarating ways to climb a mountain in the Lake District, and beats Striding Edge for danger and excitement – Sharp Edge is a notorious accident black spot which the local mountain rescue team are very familiar with. Thankfully, on the day that I chose to tiptoe along the arête, weather conditions were perfect. Crisp cold air attacked my nostrils and the sky was the bluest shade of brilliant blue I could have wished for. Having arrived via Souther Fell and the path above the River Glenderamackin, I paused at Scales Tarn and gazed upwards. Sharp Edge was like a siren's call which I willingly followed. As I began my traverse, it was as if the world fell silent. I was alone in a high place, and it was marvellous. I moved confidently across the Edge, slowing my pace to savour the moment. There is one difficult spot about mid-way along where countless thousands of bottoms have smoothed the surface and requires cautious footing – I certainly wouldn't like to cross it after it has been raining. I edged along it and found myself breathing again after I was back on solid, grippy rock. At the end of the ridge lies Foule Crag. It's an almost vertical scramble which needs to be surmounted before the summit of Blencathra can be attained. I scampered up it like a monkey, not slowing until I was on the top and making my way towards the cairn. I walked along the saddle of Saddleback, and couldn't help feeling sorry for poor Blencathra – your pseudonym is, I hate to admit it, plain silly. Even the Ordnance Survey folk can't make up their mind, as they put both names on my map (just in case). The summit has spectacular views over the Lakes, and it was no wonder that people were now swarming to it like worker ants from every direction. I was very proud of having arrived there by way of Sharp Edge. I felt I was surely able to consider myself a 'proper walker' now. The Munros can't be any harder than Blencathra and Sharp Edge, right?

Having drunk my fill of the summit and tipsy with excitement, I meandered back across the saddle, passing the mysterious large white cross on route. I followed the path to Atkinson Pike and descended down the western side. It was a stark contrast to the sunny eastern side for the sun had not yet warmed the flanks and the descent was icy. I half slithered, half skated down to the grassy plateau below, and began to trudge my way across to the summit of the much maligned Mungrisdale Common. Along with Armboth Fell, quiet and unassuming Mungrisdale Common has to be one of the most verbally abused fell in all seven of Wainwright's *Pictorial Guides*. Insults are hurled at it from every direction – why is it in the list? Why is it so dull? Why is it so wet? Why did Wainwright include it at all when he has nothing positive to say about it? Readers, I have to admit that I am fond of Mungrisdale Common. It might be wet and ever so slightly boggy, but you have to cover some damn fine walking country to reach the summit, and are rewarded with a spectacular panoramic view of the northern fells, dominated by the glorious Blencathra and the mighty Skiddaw. For those reasons I feel that Mungrisdale Common rightfully deserves a place in the *Pictorial Guides.*

As I left Mungrisdale Common and walked across the col towards Bannerdale Crags, Sharp Edge was silhouetted against the sky, with miniscule figures treading softly along the arête. It didn't seem possible that I too had conquered the fearsome edge only a few hours earlier. Time passes strangely in Lakeland. After lunching on Bannerdale Crags I walked around the crags from which the fell take its name, and headed towards Bowscale Fell and immortality. Not my own, I hasten to add, but the immortality of two fish said to forever reside in the murky depths of Bowscale Tarn. William Wordsworth referred to the fish in his poetry, but they haven't yet achieved the same level of fame as the Ullswater daffodils. I'm quite partial to a bit of fish and chips, which is perhaps why the fish never rose to the surface to greet me. Despite suffering from the disappointment of not seeing any talking trout, I feel magnanimous enough to comment that Bowscale Fell boasts a shapely cairn and large shelter in case of bad weather.

Bad weather did not feature that day, and there was not a single fluffy cloud in the sky. Diligent readers who are familiar with the Wainwright fells in the northern part of the Lake District might have spotted that there is a fell in the top north-eastern corner which I hadn't yet climbed. That fell was Carrock Fell. I had tried to climb Carrock Fell once before, but the ferocity of the wind had buffeted me about so much that I abandoned my attempt (and I hadn't moved more than five feet from the car!) That day, I went on to climb Raven Crag instead. This day, however, boasted such perfect conditions that in true 'one girl' style, I persuaded my chauffeur (once again the ever encouraging dad) to drive around to the delightfully named 'Apronful of Stones', from which I could nimbly step up Carrock Fell by way of Rake Trod. Rake Trod, though short, is steep and eroded, and I found myself clinging to the heather beside the path to heave myself upwards (side note: heather must have extremely strong roots). Once the rake has been negotiated, it is a simple but rocky route to the summit, which is a fascinating plateau of ancient Iron Age hill forts and structures long since abandoned, making Carrock Fell summit one of the most visually interesting of the Wainwright fells. The famous Victorian novelists Charles Dickens and Wilkie Collins also climbed Carrock Fell together as part of their sojourn around Cumberland. I don't think Wilkie Collins was a fan, as he sprained his ankle on the summit and had to limp back down. Literary Lakeland strikes again!

After the excitement of my Blencathra jaunt, six days lapsed before I next obeyed the call of the mountains. Good weather taunted me as I worked, and I gazed out of the windows longingly, chomping at the bit all the while. Plan after plan raced through my head as I decided which fells to tackle next, yet one option stood out head and shoulders above the rest – the chance to complete one of the *Pictorial Guides*. Believe it or not, but I had managed to climb one hundred and sixty of Wainwright's fells without managing to finish a single book. This had to change. With this in mind, I focused my plans and zoomed in on three fells: Grisedale Pike, Hopegill Head, and Whiteside. I saw nobody at all during my ascent of Grisedale Pike, and the clouds rumbled ominously above me as I gained height above Kinn and Sleet How. A biting wind chased me off the shale summit and around onto Hopegill Head as fast as my feet could go. I looked down upon Hobcarton Crag, which is a dramatic, forbidding piece of Lakeland scenery that dwarfs Hobcarton Gill, acting more like a hobgoblin than a hob-crag. Looking north across to Ladyside Pike from Hopegill Head, the path looked deliciously stony and scree-y rolled into one. I put that one on my mental 'to do' list and set off for Whiteside. The ridge route between Hopegill Head and Whiteside must be one of the very best in the Lake District. Narrow, precipitous, with tricky sections and grand views, I'm sure many would agree that it ranks up there with Striding Edge. Not as famous, certainly, but almost as good. I reached the summit of Whiteside, my fist punched the air and I rejoiced at the completion of my first book, *The North Western Fells*. As I danced around the summit, two men approached me, having reached Whiteside via Whin Ben (this was to be my descent route). They looked mightily confused to see me on the summit, for their faces showed that they had presumed themselves to be the first explorers on the summit that day. You have to get up earlier than that, gents, to get the fells to yourself – after all, it's the early bird that catches the worm.

This particular bird was after more than three worms today, and so after descending to Lanthwaite Green I went in search of worm number four, which was to prove especially juicy. Of all the Wainwrights under two thousand feet in height, Mellbreak must have one of the most, if not *the* most, difficult ascent routes. My mood was buoyant, but it soon deflated as I heaved my way up the excessively steep scree-filled north end of the fell. Perhaps I missed the intended route, for I found myself in improbably sheer gullies with earth crumbling about me as my feet scrabbled about for a purchase and paths criss-crossing all the time. It still gives me shivers just thinking about it. Plans to return that way were quickly scrapped, and I was grateful to reach the north top. On distinctly firmer ground my feet took me across to the southern top (approximately ten feet higher than the north) and I formulated a new plan. I returned to the centre of the saddle and walked down the western side of Mellbreak towards the Mosedale Holly Tree. The tree has the singular distinction of being the only lone tree indicated and named on Ordnance Survey maps in the Lake District, which is enough to make it quite a celebrity in these parts. Expect a film and book deal to be announced soon – 'The Muse of Mosedale' perhaps, or 'One Tree and the Wainwrights'. I followed Mosedale Beck back to the iconic Loweswater red phone box. Apologies to dad, who was watching the northern end of Mellbreak intently with his binoculars to see me descend, and was wondering why it was taking me so long to retrace my steps when I nonchalantly appeared beside the car. Mellbreak was a good beast to have conquered today. And my first book finished, too.

The fells at the back o' Skiddaw are shy and retiring, never asking or demanding much of anybody's time or effort. It is safe to say that you are not going to find scary ridges or famous peaks in the area known as the Uldale Fells. Favourably, the latter point also means that you are not going to find hoards of Lake District day trippers either, only the few walkers who crave solitude and peace among gentle summits. For that reason, I chose to walk the Uldale Fells as a stark contrast to the classic Lakeland terrain encountered the previous day. Most walkers who aim to climb all of the Wainwrights probably ascend all of these fells in one day due to their relatively close proximity to each other, and I was no different. My day began near the small hamlet of Longlands, and which saw me ambling up to the summits of Longlands Fell, Brae Fell, Great Sca Fell, Knott, Meal Fell, and Great Cockup. Each fell was grassy and soft and a delight to walk upon. Scenery was bleak but full of colour in the sunshine, and my heart was light. Between Longlands Fell and Brae Fell is Charleton Gill, a gash in the scenery and what dad called 'the wasteland'. I'm sure that T. S. Eliot would be pleased. Great Sca Fell is a very powerful name for a fell, although I feel brother Scafell Pike would be disappointed to meet its small relation. Little Sca Fell, although not a Wainwright, had a much more impressive cairn and a better view than Great Sca Fell. Perhaps they should swap when nobody's looking. My next fell, Knott, was knott like Great Sca Fell at all, being peaty and boggy with a moon crater-like plateau on the top. It was the only fell on this walk which strayed from the grassy hill template, and the variation was pleasing underfoot. Lunchtime soon approached, and with it the appropriately named Meal Fell.

A strange cloud formation chased me over to Meal Fell, and I was grateful to huddle in the shelter and devour my sandwiches. Maybe it was my appetite chasing me over the fell tops, as once I had consumed my dinner the eerie mist had disappeared. I danced with the troubadours down to Trusmadoor (I can't help it, Trusmadoor sounds so very jolly) and up to the summit of Great Cockup. Great Cockup, I am ashamed to say, was indeed the site of a great cock-up. I had enjoyed a pleasant walk and planned to descend over the nose of the fell towards Orthwaite Bank. For some reason, after phoning my chauffeur (dad), I followed his advice to follow a path which was very vague on the ground but very clear when seen from a distance (pater had binoculars). I followed the new path down to where it fizzled out into nothing, had to follow a wall along for what seemed to be a very long distance, splashed through innumerable puddles, avoided innumerable horseflies, and emerged at the road thoroughly grumpy and unimpressed, having walked for far longer than I had intended due to the unplanned detour. Let us just say that the atmosphere in the car was tense. My only explanation is that I was tired, and for that I heartily apologise. However, I wasn't grouchy enough to ignore the delights of the fabulously pink Orthwaite Hall or consume a chocolatey peace-offering. My bad-temper melted into good humour very quickly, and I swiftly decided that Great Cockup has one of the very best, and most apt, fell names in the whole of the Lake District.

Unlikely pairings of fells are one of the interesting features of completing the Wainwrights. Usually we choose to climb mountains that are situated next to each other, for ease of access more than anything else, yet my next walk paired two single fells that are separated by some distance. I wanted to 'pick them off', as it were, and a short drive was necessary to link the two. Both were great. Quite literally, in fact, as the two were Great Crag and Great Calva, from *The Central Fells* and *The Northern Fells* respectively. The route up Great Crag meanders up towards Lingy End, passing White Crag and emerging at the beautiful Dock Tarn, with reeds gently swaying in the breeze. I walked in circles to find the summit as it is not obvious from the tarn, but I eventually emerged triumphant, and surveyed Lakeland looking glorious in the November sunshine. Great Crag is a patchwork quilt of a fell, with heather, rocks, peat, grass and water all gracing its flanks, and has the honour of finishing the *Central Fells* for me. Great Calva is much bleaker, with a dark peaty surface and only a little heather struggling for life. My ascent of Great Calva from Dash Falls by Dry Gill was incredibly steep, and I'm glad that the fence posts were strong as I had to hold onto them on more than one occasion. After a very short time on the summit I returned the way I had come, tipping Little Calva my invisible hat in farewell as I passed. Despite the sunshine it was bitterly cold and the light was fading, and I had to abandon my additional plan of scaling Bakestall the same day. Never mind, the fells will await my return!

Alas, the fells waited a very long time before I returned. The harshness of winter arrived and my muddy boots entered hibernation as winter festivities took priority over conquering mountains. In the meantime, I moved away from the Lake District and my beloved fells. I knew that completing the Wainwrights would be that much harder now I had to travel three hours every time I wanted to climb the Lakeland fells. You will read how I made every effort to eke out as many fells as possible in one day whenever I ventured northwards. Life often gets in the way of ambition, but I was determined not to let distance slow me in my tracks.

When the last throes of winter wrestled with spring, I emptied tumbleweed from the pockets of my waterproof coat and trusty trousers and headed out into the mountains. What followed was a walk which has long stayed in my memory. What the walk also gave me was the opportunity to use a greater and wide-ranging selection of adjectives, as my traverse of Clough Head and the Dodds was the only true winter walk that I undertook during my Wainwright quest. I felt like a true arctic explorer! As we drove through the Lake District, I was nervous as I saw the amount of snow on the fell tops. I worried that it would be slippery with poor visibility, and before I left Wanthwaite along the old coach road I decided that if I was not happy with the conditions I would retrace my steps. I climbed up into the cloud past the snow line, and into a world of ice. There were no footsteps in the snow before me, and so I blazed a path towards the summit of Clough Head.

The scenery took my breath away. Shining icicles froze motionless on the cairn, and delicate hoarfrost covered the trig point. It was spectacular. All thoughts of turning back left me, and I plunged onwards, excited and exhilarated. Glittering snow troughs covered the ground so that paths were non-existent, and I navigated my way to Great Dodd using my compass. Just when I thought I may have gone wrong, Great Dodd's cairn lumbered out of the snowy cloud towards me. I removed my mittens to take a photograph and retrieve a snack from my rucksack but soon thought better of it as my hands turned pink with cold. Watson's Dodd followed, then Stybarrow Dodd (an old friend from long ago), and Hart Side after that. The ground was frozen in part and my feet crunched across the plateau with satisfying noises. In other areas a powdery soft snow tricked my unwary feet and I plunged knee deep into drifts. It was marvellous. I forgot about the ditch on Hart Side's summit and promptly walked straight over it, falling into a graceful giggling heap in the snow (it's a good job there were no other walkers around to see my seasonal madness).

Dazzling whiteness shone into my eyes and I was glad that my sunglasses, a lone remnant of summer walking attire, were still in my rucksack. As I moved down towards Sheffield Pike, I met more walkers coming up who were dressed very differently to me. I wore trousers, base layer tops, mid-layers, a fleece, waterproof coat, hat, and mittens.

Some were ascending in tee-shirts! Hopefully they had more layers stashed away for when they crossed into the frozen wastelands. I must have appeared like a yeti, for I received some curious looks as I sat on the summit of Sheffield Pike, admiring Ullswater. The sun was out and with gleeful steps I moved onwards (or rather downwards – it felt strange to have to descend to claim a Wainwright) to Glenridding Dodd, which was my final fell from *The Eastern Fells.* I've never yet described a fell as being 'cute', but Glenridding Dodd might just be the one. With shining eyes and a big smile I walked down to my waiting chauffeur, thinking that today must rank as one of my top mountain days so far. Long may they last! It was the experience rather than the achievement which was the highlight of this walk, particularly as I was a girl alone in the wintery wildness, and a novice winter walker to boot. I hope other girls are encouraged to follow in my snowy footsteps – Bigfoot's got nothing on me.

I completed *The Northern Fells* in my next walk, with the steep ascent up Birkett Edge to Bakestall a severe warm up for my muscles at eight o'clock in the morning. Tempting though Skiddaw was, I resisted her call and stuck to the plan. Note to self: wear in new walking boots gently. I switched to my old faithfuls for the next section of the day, which promised a gentle jaunt around three westerly Wainwrights – Gavel Fell, Blake Fell, and Burnbank Fell. They did not disappoint. With cheerful skies, a cheerful mind, and a cheerful rucksack (a new piece of kit – bright yellow – which put a smile on my face every time I glanced its way) I set off from Maggie's Bridge. I don't know who Maggie is, but she picked a lovely spot for a bridge. The beautiful Loweswater was all too soon left behind as I proceed up and over the nose of Gavel Fell and followed the gently meandering path to its summit. Two startled black grouse sprang up in front of me and whirred away into the distance, squawking angrily at the disruption of their countryside retreat. It was a magical moment, and I savoured it as I sat by the summit cairn. Blake Fell soon followed, with a bird's eye view of the deforested Knock Murton. Next stop was Burnbank Fell. Burnbank Fell is one of those interesting little fells which has a small cairn, but whose true summit is a fencepost. That is, the fencepost stands on the true summit. Hartsop Dodd is another. I could tell that many other walkers had posed in that particular corner of the fence, as the grass was worn away to dust. After drinking in more of the March sunshine I gambolled down to Holme Wood, using the terrace paths to bring me back to enchanting Loweswater.

Following the now well-established 'one girl' style, there was time to fit in one more Wainwright before home beckoned. Hen Comb was chosen, and I fear there was some foul play afoot (oh dear) as it took me an awful long time to reach the comb of the fell. (For those not poultry-minded, a comb is the red protuberance on the head of birds such as chickens and turkeys, and is possibly where the insult 'coxcomb' derives from.) Etymological considerations aside, however, I shall return to my walk. Perhaps it was my tired legs, perhaps it was the lazy late afternoon sun, perhaps it was the fact my stash of chocolate had run out, perhaps it was a combination of all three, but I was mighty glad to reach the grassy summit of Hen Comb and have a much longed-for rest. Either way, I was soon refreshed and ambled down the fell, clucking gaily to myself all the way to Loweswater village and the red phone box. After a refreshing paddle in Park Beck to cool my tired and hot feet, it was time to head home.

Well-worn summit fence post on Burnbank Fell

There are some fells which are friends, and some which are foes. One particular mountain is neither, as I consider him to be a formidable adversary who twice defied me, and only on the third attempt did I manage to scale his rocky heights. Three is indeed a lucky number for me where Wetherlam is concerned. On my first attempt, we thought and discussed and cogitated but in the end the Coniston bus timetables were against us, and we had to leave Wetherlam for another day. On my second attempt, I was forced back by the elements. The day started innocently enough with a few clouds but nothing unduly worrying about the conditions. I wound my way up to the Coppermines Valley and headed for Levers Water. As I approached Swirl Hawse the weather took a turn for the worse. Waterproofs were donned in vain, for heavy splodges of the wettest type of rain burst upon my head. The monsoon continued, and the wind joined in. Howling thrusts of air pummelled my body, and I crouched behind a rock for shelter. Sensing a lull in the weather I inched forwards, only to be repelled once more. Rain turned to hail, and my cheeks stung with the violence of storm. Visibility was severely reduced. I knew my limits, and could not tell how far I was from the summit. I backed down and stumbled down the mountain, tail between my legs and disappointed at having so narrowly missed a Wainwright. I rested next to Levers Water, propped up by a reassuringly large boulder. As I gazed out at the rough waves, I noticed a very curious thing. There appeared to be a column of water hovering on the surface, seemingly made up of water whipped up by the fierce winds.

"Wow", I thought to myself, "I never thought I'd see a waterspout in the Lake District, of all places."

A second thought came to me.

"But that waterspout's not moving. I've heard that if you're looking at a tornado, and the tornado's not moving, then it's coming straight at you. If that's true, then that waterspout must be – oh no!"

In no time at all, the waterspout was upon me. I had no time to move and could only put my arms over my head, curl up into a ball, and hope for the best. My next sensation was as though somebody up in the sky had upturned a whole bathtub of cold water onto my head. The waterspout disintegrated upon impact, and I sat there, shivering and dazed. I realise that it probably wasn't a true waterspout that formed there in Levers Water as it wasn't connected to a cloud, but it was a strange experience, and one that I won't be forgetting in a hurry. I must have appeared a sorry sight to walkers as I squelched down in my wet clothes and saturated boots. Back in Coniston, the sun was shining. Typical.

On my third attempt to conquer the sleeping giant of Wetherlam, I succeeded. Conditions were just right. The familiar territory of Levers Water was gained, quickly followed by Swirl Hawse. Next came the push for the summit. Triumphant, I approached the cairn. No Wainwright had been fought for so hard as I had fought for Wetherlam, and my efforts were finally rewarded. I gave a cheer, and ate a victorious jam sandwich. I descended to Hole Rake, nodded a 'how d'you do' to a passing fell runner, and made my way to the car, where I could report success for the day's mission. The day's mission, however, was only half completed. The next stop was Wastwater. After a shaky start (narrow, winding roads can make me distinctly queasy if I am not driving) I set off to climb alongside Greathall Gill to Whin Rigg. Dancing round some jumpy-looking cows, I moved up the fell side. The view backwards over Wastwater was definitely preferable to the view in front up the steep slope. With steely determination I made it up to the summit of Whin Rigg, and stared awestruck at the sheer drop down the screes. A never-ending waterfall of rocks streamed into the water below, and I felt impossibly high. I was thoroughly enjoying myself, yet the ridge route between Whin Rigg and Illgill Head must be sorely underappreciated. Most other walkers were taking the 'straight as the crow flies' route between the two summits. Not me. I took the winding cliff path which meanders in and out of all the nooks and crannies of the

Rivers of scree flowing into Wastwater

cliff edge. The views were nothing short of wondrous and I (possibly due to giddy elation) abandoned all sense of safety and stuck my foot over the edge of the cliff, as if to prove to myself that, yes, I really was there standing on the shoulders of giants.

There were plenty of other fell walkers around, but only a tiny proportion were walking the same path as myself. I collared one such walker for a photo opportunity, who commented that "The only downside of solo walking is having to ask other people to take your photograph." I disagree, as it's an opportunity to reach out to fellow walkers, exchange a few pleasantries, and move on feeling enamoured of the human race. Walkers are, in general, a friendly folk. Illgill Head proved this, as I had an animated discussion with a chap who had the same bright bumblebee yellow rucksack as myself, and we contentedly talked litres and packs and gear until the path lured me onwards. I caught a glimpse of Burnmoor Tarn as I descended, and formulated another plan to walk around every single tarn and lake within the Lake District. I'll save that for another book, perhaps. Next stop was the car park at Brackenclose, and I slowed my feet to savour the walk. It was, after all, a long drive home.

Long drives to and from the Lake District affect me in different ways. Sometimes I savour the journey, eagerly alert for the first sighting of the fells in the distance. Other times I sleep, tired from the early start. If I am not driving my own car, I can get a little car-sick (hence my impressions of a dog with its head hanging out of the window, as I like the fresh air). On one particular occasion, my stomach did not agree with the tiny, windy roads towards Wasdale, no not at all. I had enough warning to produce a faint gurgling sound, rapidly wind down the window and half stick my head out before I vomited down the side of the car. It was not pretty. White-faced, I looked up and saw the car behind us using its windscreen wipers.

"It's not raining, why is the car behind washing its windows?" I asked my ever-supportive dad.

Straight-faced, but trying not to laugh, he replied, "Your sick sprayed over his windscreen so he had to clean it."

Oh my. Driver of the black car, wherever you are, I am so sorry for the spattering of sick on your windscreen. I hope you will forgive me in the knowledge that in was in pursuit of the Wainwrights that your car was dirtied.

A small voice piped up from the back seat. "You didn't manage to send it all out of the car, either. I have sick on my foot!" Poor mum, you too suffered from my travel sickness. It was weeks before the smell went away.

Nevertheless, despite such an unpromising start I completed another of my greatest fell walks that day, crossing from Wasdale to Ennerdale and taking in the summits of Pillar, Red Pike, Scoat Fell, Steeple, Haycock and Caw Fell along the way. A magnificent walk which I thoroughly recommend. First stop of the day was the mighty Pillar, formidable denizen of Cumbria, famed far and wide for the climbing country around Pillar Rock. My ascent took the way of the Black Sail Pass onto the ridge, climbing upwards to greet the summit. Yellowhammers flitted around me, alighting on rocks and quickly shooting off again, seemingly leading me ever onwards. Gatherstone Beck was gorged from recent heavy rain, and it was with difficulty that I crossed the watery barrier. A sweet little black lamb wobbled along the path in front of me, stopping and gazing at the huge lumbering creature approaching it. It was not afraid of me and so I sashayed around it, careful not to startle the woolly individual. The summit of Pillar is a broad plateau which is disconcertingly flat. After the climb I expected sharpness and shapeliness, but the expansive summit felt rather too civilised for my liking. I moved to the edge and gazed down at the hulking mass of Pillar Rock, immortalised by Wordsworth in the poem, *The Brothers.*

Red Pike was up next. I negotiated the rather steep obstacle of Wind Gap (no wind, though) and made my way to the summit. Red Pike's cairn is situated on the very edge of the cliff, providing a good vantage point to view Mosedale below. Best not to linger if it's windy. I spied some patches of the red clay from which, I can only presume, Red Pike got its name, and was thankful that today's Red Pike was much less eventful than the Buttermere Red Pike of yore (for those who can't recall that particular incident, it is fondly remembered as 'The Death Ascent').

Endearingly, I always think of the next summit of the day as being called 'Stoat Fell', due to me misreading the fell's name when I first perused *The Western Fells*. 'Scoat Fell' is, however disappointingly correct, and as I suspected, there were no stoats dancing around the cairn. Indeed, 'Scoat Fell' may be the best name for the fell, as the meaning of 'scoat' is 'to prop', which is exactly what Scoat Fell does to its cairn. A lengthy dry stone wall (known as the 'Ennerdale Fence') runs for a long distance over the summits of the fells, and Scoat Fell's cairn sits directly on top of it, straddling the wall. An enterprising solution for when the summit of the fell is already occupied by a wall, and so the wall props up the cairn. Scoat Fell is nothing if not quirky. The next mountain on my agenda is one of the best in the Lake District: Steeple. A short hop, skip and a jump away from Scoat Fell, it is fantastically rocky, pointy, and packs a punch for its diminutive size. I loved it. However, Steeple's charms mean that other people love it too, and I shared the shapely summit with a middle-aged couple, two curious black Labradors who hopefully sniffed at my rucksack (nothing in there for you, cheeky), and three chaps who hogged the cairn. I would definitely like to return to Steeple, possibly walking directly from the Ennerdale Forest up to the summit (and choosing an early morning to have the mountain to myself!)

My next stop on the Wainwright train was Haycock, followed by Caw Fell. Navigation is incredibly easy between these two, only requiring you to follow the dry stone wall along and halt where you wish to halt. As the distance increased between myself and Steeple, the people became fewer. Haycock is another moonscape-like summit, with many sharp rocks protruding from the grass to trip up unwary walkers. Caw Fell, despite being equally as rocky around the cairn, feels much smoother and velvety in character. This is perhaps due to the sheer sense of isolation you get when standing on the summit of Caw Fell – it must be one of the loneliest summits in Lakeland. I enjoyed the remoteness of the spot, until I realised that it was still quite some distance to the waiting car. Heaving up my rucksack with a sigh, I began the steady plod down to the car park near Bowness Knott. For anybody who saw a strange girl doing bird impressions on the nose of Caw Fell that day, I can offer no apologies. The very name of Caw Fell insists that I caw as loudly as I can in honour of the name of the fell, so that is what I did. I threw in some arm flapping for good measure, too. On a more mundane note, whilst on my descent, I passed moorland, heather, forest, river and lakeside (on second thoughts, how can these ever be described as mundane? The scenery was beautiful and invigorating to walk through.) The sun was shining and a canoeist on Ennerdale Water complimented the scene. There was nothing I wanted more than a swim in the lake to cool my body, but I resisted. Soggy clothes in the car on the way home would not be pleasant.

Discovering secret valleys and hidden treasures is one of the best aspects of walking all of the two hundred and fourteen fells in Wainwright's *Pictorial Guides.* Possibly the most delightful valley in the whole of the Lake District is shy Longsleddale, where I began my next walk. Longsleddale is a long, winding, gorgeously pretty valley which snakes its way into the fells in the far eastern side of the national park. The valley also supposedly inspired Postman Pat's home of Greendale, and Longsleddale is indeed lusciously green and pleasant. It even boasts a fantastic set of public toilets, complete with pictures on the walls and a visitors' book (which, of course, I duly signed). My motive for entering beautiful Longsleddale was to finish off *The Far Eastern Fells*, as I had only the quartet of Grey Crag, Tarn Crag, Branstree and Selside Pike left in that particular book. Starting from the old packhorse bridge at Sadgill, I wound my way up the fellside and onto the glorious bleak moorland which is more akin to the Pennines than the Lake District. Standing

Let the bog-hopping commence

by the summit cairn of Grey Crag, I surveyed the route to Tarn Crag, which takes a direct line through an area known ominously as Greycrag Tarn.

Thankfully, Greycrag Tarn was more like a very peaty bog than a watery tarn, although I've no doubt the further you stray to the west the more watery the ground would get. I leapt from tussock to tussock, stone to stone, hump to hump, climbing over the fence every now and again to achieve firmer ground. It was great fun, but I was very pleased to be out of the squelch and onto the summit. Tarn Crag has a neat little cairn, but the distinctive feature of the summit is a huge surveying column which was used to help build the Haweswater aqueduct. I walked its full circumference before setting off in hot pursuit of Branstree. Whilst descending to the col, I invented a new Olympic sport: peat surfing. You step on a loose section of peat (accidentally or on purpose, I began with the former) and surf elegantly down the fell side. I've yet to discover if you can perform any tricks whilst peat surfing, so the aerials and cross steppings (manoeuvres favoured by the more usual type of surfer) will have to await further investigation.

Branstree, like Blencathra, has a dog bowl on the summit. By this I mean it has a circular band which is useful for storing rainwater for thirsty animals, but which is in fact a flat trig point. Moving on to the twin cairns of Artlecrag Pike (not a Wainwright) I chatted to a couple who, after their walk, were going to watch a duck race in Bampton (there would be more than one duck present). It just goes to show that you only hear of interesting things if you take the time to talk to people. After admiring the glorious views over Haweswater towards the High Street range, I followed the fence to Selside Pike. The terrifyingly named 'Captain Welter Bog' wasn't in the least alarming, for which I was grateful, and Selside Pike has an ample shelter in which to recline and contemplate the day. It was extremely pleasant in the midday sun, and I had to stop myself from having a quick snooze! My tired legs took me down the nose of the fell to join the Old Corpse Road, where I made a sharp left and began my descent. Just to the side of the path was an intriguing area fenced off with ropes, which after investigation proved to be a deep bog hole which was ringed off to prevent unwary walkers from falling in. I followed the path all the way down to Haweswater and another successful fell walking day ended, with my fifth *Pictorial Guide* completed too.

Roman occupation seems to feature fairly often when walking the Wainwrights. High Street jumps immediately to mind, and there is a Roman fort in Ambleside too. One of the most striking Roman strongholds is Hardknott Roman fort, which is a very remote fort situated next to the Hardknott Pass road near Eskdale. Walls and rooms still exist, and you can march around and pretend to be a Roman soldier on parade. During my next walk I looked down onto the fort many times, which showed the remaining structures off to their full advantage. I had selected three fells, one of which has as its namesake the aforementioned fort. The chosen three were Hard Knott, Harter Fell, and Green Crag. Hard Knott is a grand little fell which packs a punch for its small size, as it has fantastic views over the Scafell massif. I don't know if the television reception is particularly poor around this area, but somebody had stuck an aerial in the top of the cairn. Let's call it modern art and leave it at that. Anyway, a quick little out-and-back from the top of the pass saw me knobble Hard Knott. Not so hard now, eh?

I crossed the road and began the steady ascent up Harter Fell. Harter Fell has a wondrous summit that belongs within the realms of fantasy fiction. The rocky pinnacle is split in two like a gigantic Arnison Crag. Unsure of whether it was the trig point, the cairned area, or the other high rocky tor which marked the summit I climbed all three and had a jolly good explore. The fell boasts extensive views over Green Crag, Ulpha Fell and into Dunnerdale and the Duddon Valley, and is a perfect base for exploring other fells around Eskdale. I shall now abandon my attempt at estate-agent talk, and move on to my third and final fell of the day, Green Crag. I will freely admit that I was slightly afraid of the route across to Green Crag, as I had read about bogginess and wetness and sliminess. Happily, I experienced none of this. The path was firm if a little peaty, and when it petered out (again, sorry) I blazed a trail directly towards Green Crag, suffering no ill effects in the process. However, I would advise great caution if contemplating this route in heavy mist. The summit was calming and peaceful, and I enjoyed the solitude, the silence, and the sound of humming bees. All too soon I left the fell, winding my way down to

Doctor Bridge where I glimpsed my third red squirrel (third in my life, not third of the day, which would be far too greedy). What is interesting about today's three fells is that I saw not a single other soul for the entire duration of my walk. Not even a tiny figure on the horizon! I knew that these fells are traversed much less frequently than the tourist honey pots like Fairfield, Scafell Pike and Helvellyn, but I had expected to see at least a couple of other peak-baggers in the area. Let us say that I fondly recalled the isolation on this walk during an encounter with the frenzied madding crowds on a future sunny hike to the summit of Scafell Pike.

But before I scaled the highest peak in England, I climbed a fair few other Wainwrights first. As I walk, for the most part, on my own, I do enjoy having the company of other people, especially people who make for laughter and jokes among the way. It is with great pleasure, therefore, that I reintroduce to the scene the three musketeers – EJ, JM, and myself. We decided that it was high time we went on another trip, which is promptly what we did. Youth hostels booked, we met up in the Lakes once again. As I was now the proud owner of my very first car, I was the transport officer for the trip, and picked the other two musketeers up from the train station and drove us around to Stonethwaite where we began the day's hike. Our aim was Rosthwaite Fell and the enchantingly named summit, Bessyboot. We climbed up alongside Big Stanger Gill and entered a strange world. JM rightly described the fell as exotic, and I thoroughly agree. The air turned hot, sweaty and humid. Large flies danced around us. Water glistened on ferns. It was like we had entered the Jurassic age. We followed the gently wandering path along and around lumps, bumps and humps before climbing triumphantly to the top of Bessyboot. Resting at the immensely scenic Tarn at Leaves, we explored the fell a little before deciding to descend as it was growing late and we need to check in to our youth hostel in Keswick. We were right to do so. The very moment that we headed down near Rottenstone Gill was the very moment that the weather turned rotten to match. Rain lashed against our clothes, our feet sloshed around in our boots and within seconds we were soaked to the skin. We squelched back to Stonethwaite and the waiting car. Fortunately we all had changes of clothes and after a few furtive looks around we speedily changed into our dry clothes with nothing but towels to hide our modesty. Shortly after, two male walkers passed by. If they had arrived a few seconds earlier they would have seen a sight not readily forgotten. Three girls wriggling under towels in a vain attempt to become warm again, flinging wet walking gear around and laughing uncontrollably. They say laughter is medicine for the soul – I wholeheartedly agree.

Rosthwaite Fell was my two hundredth Wainwright.

After a night eating fish and chips, playing snooker and exploring our youth hostel, we were soon in the car and driving around to one of the most secluded areas in the Lake District – the wild Ennerdale valley.

THE FINAL FOURTEEN

It is with a heightened sense of anticipation that I write this chapter, for it heralds the final countdown to mountain number two hundred and fourteen. No peeking (you know who you are). It won't be long before the champagne is cracked open and my journey is at an end.

I drove my tiny little car along the forest road beside Ennerdale Water, manoeuvring this way and that to avoid the potholes. Successfully averting the chances of a punctured tyre, we parked up at the youth hostel, who were happy to let the car stay put as we were sleeping there that night. So far so good. What I have omitted to mention is the solid globules of water pelting out of the sky. Let me tell you that it is a struggle to put on full waterproofs when seated in a small three-door car, and even harder with a steering wheel in front of you. Squirming like worms and writhing like snakes we somehow managed it, and set forth into the rain and up alongside Gillflinter Beck. Our first fell of the day was to be Starling Dodd, which was the last fell Wainwright ascended during his thirteen-year expedition to write the *Pictorial Guides*. Onwards and upwards into the mist we went, careful to head to the west and Starling Dodd rather than to the east and Red Pike – we didn't want to encounter that particular fell again (see our earlier experiences of the latter fell previously recorded in this book). The summit cairns on Starling Dodd are twofold, as one is traditional stone and the other consists of twisting metal fence posts. Both provide scant shelter, as we found to our cost when trying to huddle behind them from the howling winds and the biting chill. A flock of starlings flew around the cairns in a desperate attempt to hide from the elements. I jest, of course. Yet again fell names were proving contradictory, and there were no starlings to be seen on, in, or around Starling Dodd. It was clearly time to move on to Great Borne.

The path to Great Borne produced one of the best moments of my fell walking career to date. As we approached the fence which we were to follow to the summit of Great Borne, something moved in the corner of our eyes. A small, struggling black lamb was caught in the metal fence wire. Somehow the woolly individual had managed to wiggle his head into the fence, and due to his growing horns couldn't pull himself back out again. Each time he tried, the horns would jam up against the wire. His mother was nowhere in sight and it was clear that he was scared. There was no time to lose. The three musketeers to the rescue! Dropping our rucksacks and hurrying forward, we began our rescue mission. I seized the body of the lamb, gripping tightly to prevent any movement (and to stop the lamb from pushing forwards, which would make it difficult to free his head). JM and EJ jointly contrived to push the lamb's head down and to one side, freeing one horn. The second horn quickly followed, notwithstanding the lamb's vain efforts to break free from us as the poor thing didn't realising that we were helping. One, two, freedom! William Wallace could not have felt prouder at that moment than we did. The lamb stumbled backwards, and looked us in the eye. We stared back, relieved to have saved him from starvation. A few seconds more, and he happily gambolled down the fell, hopefully to rejoin his flock. We named him Herdus (chosen in honour of his breed, Herdwick, and the name of a small fell we were to descend by later in the walk). It was with pride that we watched him go, and our adrenaline powered us up the flank of Great Borne.

Standing next to the trig point on the summit of Great Borne, we truly felt that it was a great day. Our feet fairly floated along the ground for the rest of the day, so happy were we to have freed the little black lamb. Baa, baa, black sheep, you may have left some wool on the metal fence as you gaily tripped away, but you were free to go and deliver more to the master, the dame, and the little boy who lives down the lane. Meanwhile, the trio of adventurers set off down the fellside, said hello to a frog on the way, and reached Ennerdale Water with much laughter. What followed was a beautifully scenic meander along the forest road back to the youth hostel. A wholesome and hearty evening meal provided the icing on the exhilarating cake that had been our day. As we relaxed in the evening no traffic disrupted our conversations and no intrusive streetlamps stole away the stars. Ennerdale youth hostel is in a truly beautiful location. We will definitely return one day!

The western side of the Lake District became the focus of my dozen remaining Wainwrights. Fells in this area are far away from any motorway, and are thus blessed from the madding crowds which surge upon Grasmere, Ambleside, Keswick and Bowness on weekends. They also boast some of the most dramatic rock scenery in the Lakes, and are home to the two highest mountains in England. The highest, Scafell Pike, was going to feature in my next walk. After a very early start we picked up RF (who hails from this beautiful part of the world) and wound our way around to Wasdale Head, where we began the walk. I had selected two fells for the day: Lingmell and Scafell Pike. Lingmell was pit stop number one. Looking backwards as we walked up the nose of Lingmell, we had fantastic views over Wasdale and Wastwater, and looking onwards Great Gable, Kirk Fell, the Mosedale horseshoe and Styhead Tarn were visible. Lingmell's cairns were very satisfactory, as one was pointy and elegantly constructed (this one had the best overall views) and the other was, quite simply, huge (the latter had an excellent vantage point for admiring the fearsome Piers Gill ravine). Whilst we moved around the summit of Lingmell, the weather drifted between rain, sunshine, and fog. The temperature moved from warm to cool to humid over and over again. Far from being irritating, the changeability of the elements only served to heighten our anticipation as we moved towards Lingmell Col and the track up to the highest mountain in England.

The moment that we joined the main path which would lead us to the summit of Scafell Pike, the whole atmosphere of the walk changed. The route became much busier and much less relaxing. We were joined by a multitude of other walkers of all shapes and sizes wearing waterproofs, jeans, shorts, and jumpers – usually in fluorescent colours which jarred harshly against the landscape. As the atmosphere of the walk changed, so did we. There was much less light-hearted chat as we put our heads down to begin the final slog up the mountain. RF suggested that an artistic liberty worth taking would be to write how we jogged quickly up to the summit of Scafell Pike. However, in the spirit of veracity, I will say that in a race between us and a snail, the snail would have won. Truthfully, to do us credit, our pace was definitely on the quick side as we moved up the mountainside. There was no question as to whether we were on the correct path or not – the steady flow of walkers passing us on their way down and the numerous cairns marking the route was knowledge enough that the highest point in England was only a short walk away. When my dad climbed Scafell Pike many years ago there were no cairns at all.

Indeed, the first time my dad made it to the summit of Scafell Pike was in thick fog with extremely poor visibility. He navigated himself and two friends from the valley of Mickleden to the summit where they enjoyed a well-deserved rest. As they reclined against the main cairn, a ghostly figure approached out of the mist. It was the leader of a trail running club, scattering pieces of paper across the mountains for a club race.

"Enjoying the mountain, lads?" he asked jovially.
"Yep – very pleased to have made it onto the summit of Scafell Pike in all this fog."
"Scafell Pike? This is Bow Fell. The Pike's over in that direction", he pointed.

My dad wasn't so sure. He'd walked all over the Lake District, and was confident in his own abilities. The paper trail leader jogged off, leaving three disappointed walkers behind him. My dad felt that he had let his friends down, and it was with dejection that he led the trio back down the mountain. Two months later, they decided to try again to reach the summit of Scafell Pike. This time, coming from Wasdale Head, they were certain they'd summitted the right mountain. As they tucked into their sandwiches, one of the three noticed a set of initials scratched into the stone of the main summit cairn. Lo and behold, it was the initials of my dad's friend, who was a compulsive carver – proof that my dad had been right all along! You can imagine the joy on his face when all three realised that this was now the second time they'd been on the summit of Scafell Pike together. My dad only wonders where on earth the trail leader got to if he thought he was on Bow Fell and was actually on Scafell Pike. The competitors must have run an extra long race that day...

RF and I too made it to the summit of Scafell Pike. Thousands have made it before us, yet it still felt special. Customary photographs were taken at the trig point and the cairn, and we retired to a distance for a spot of people watching. There were many people. Young, old, fat, thin, and mainly male walkers were milling around the summit eating, drinking, laughing, shouting and stumbling over the boulders which cover the plateau. Views were non-existent. Walking to the top of the highest mountain in England felt like a big achievement, albeit a simple one. The paths were like motorways and were very clear. To further the domesticity, someone had stuck a golf club into one of the cairns. I wonder if it will eventually rust due to the altitude? After snacking on the summit we began our descent, satisfied with our expedition. Of the two fells visited today, Lingmell was without a doubt my favourite. Lingmell was lonely and lacked the crowds of Scafell Pike. We could truly appreciate the beauty of the rugged mountains without voices chattering, food packets rustling or champagne corks popping every minute or two around us. Lingmell was heaven, Scafell Pike less so. Nevertheless, I am pleased to have conquered it.

Some mountains have harsh, unforgiving names. Scafell Pike is one such creature, with devilish undertones to match its craggy exterior. Others are gentle, with names which roll mellifluously off the tongue and are a pleasure to speak and to hear. Of the latter fells, I believe Glaramara to have one of the loveliest mountain names in the whole of the Lake District. My ascent route followed the steep Hinds Gill path, which is a little tricky to find but once found, is clear and easy to follow. Upon reaching the ridge I made a beeline for the summit and was soon king of my very own castle. Invigorated by the July sunshine I struck up a fast pace and marched on to Allen Crags, bringing back memories of climbing the fell the previous year. Esk

Hause brought on further memories, but I was jolted out of them by the many Scafell Pike-bound walkers whose company I had joined. It was refreshing to turn aside from the rushing stream and head towards Great End, receiving a few curious looks from other hikers whose facial expressions strongly suggested that they thought I was going the wrong way. I was most definitely going the right way, as Great End was the next fell on my hiking agenda.

Great End is great, and I fully understand why some hill walkers choose to save it until the end of their Wainwright quest. It certainly has the name for a final fell, that's for sure. It has great views, too. Not just great but mesmerising, as the cairns are positioned perfectly for a lunch spot with views estate agents would fight for. I was reluctant to leave the lonely summit, but had to move on, retrace my steps to Esk Hause, and pay a visit to Sprinkling Tarn. The peaceful aura of the tarn was soon shattered as a large group of schoolchildren followed me to a nearby scattering of tents. What a wonderful place for a wild camp! I lingered for a few minutes, and continued onwards to my final Wainwright of the day. Seathwaite Fell is akin to a smaller Rosthwaite Fell, with hillocks and humps and grassy knolls galore. It has three separate tops so naturally I visited all of them, startling a sheep on the way. I pioneered a descent route off the northern end of the fell alongside a gill which was very steep but which made me feel like a true Lakeland explorer. Unlacing my boots back in Seathwaite, I contemplated the fact that I was only seven fells away from completing all two hundred and fourteen described in Wainwright's *Pictorial Guides*. Smiling to myself, I began the long drive home.

August appeared, and with it came long days, masses of sunshine, bluebird skies, and plentiful fluffy clouds. Of the seven fells that I had yet to climb, every single one was based around Wasdale. Wasdale, then, was to be the location of my next hiking adventure. I chose a trio of fells for the first part of the day: Middle Fell, Seatallan, and Buckbarrow. Throughout today I was constantly reminded how the act of walking the Wainwrights is not only about the walking, although I admit that the physical act of putting one foot in front of the other does form a significant part of it. Often it is much more about the people that you meet and talk to along the way, as today's walk amply demonstrated.

I began my day alongside Greendale Gill, before branching off to follow the path up to the summit of Middle Fell. Apparently when there is no mist you can see the Scafell massif in sharp clarity from the summit. Alas I cannot vouch for this, as the mist only briefly cleared to reveal a sombre-looking Wastwater deep in the valley. Middle Fell has a sizeable cairn, which must have rested many an aching back once the stiff pull up to the summit has been completed (I was no exception). As I enjoyed my repose, a fellow walker joined me on the summit and we started chatting. He had climbed one hundred and two Wainwrights, for which I congratulated him. He then asked my tally in return. When I shyly admitted that Middle Fell was my two hundred and eighth, he was stunned. Completely taking me by surprise, he asked if he could shake my hand, as he had never met anyone who was so close to completion. He wished me luck, and I him.

Buoyant from this meeting, I sailed down the fell-side, across the col, and up to the summit of Seatallan. I'm sure that this fell deserve more exploration than I was prepared to give it, because for one very good reason I departed its summit post haste. I took the obligatory photographs and sat down next to the cairn for a chocolate-shaped snack. A fly buzzed near me. Then another one drifted past my hand. A third made a beeline for the chocolate. All at once I realised that these pesky insects were not flies but wasps! Seatallan's cairn had become one huge wasp's nest, and I could see them flying in and out of gaps in the stones. Always a courteous hiker, I gave the wasps a cheery goodbye and quickly trotted off in the direction of Buckbarrow, looking over my shoulder to check that a swarm of angry wasps wasn't sneaking up on me from behind, cartoon-style. From a distance, my actions must have looked rather peculiar. Jumping up, swatting myself, grabbing my things, running away, and looking behind. Wasps are sly creatures, you know. You can't be too careful.

Buckbarrow is a dinky little fell, a rocky knobble rather like Pike o'Stickle in miniature when viewed from the valley. The grassy walk to the summit from Seatallan across to Cat Bields and Glade How was heaven for my booted feet, and the view of The Screes from Buckbarrow's summit is mesmerising. Whilst on the summit I made the acquaintance of another hiker who arrived on the summit shortly after myself. As it turns out, he had completed exactly the same walk as me, and had the exact same plan to further scale the lofty heights of Yewbarrow the same day. Yewbarrow was part two of my day. Having thought that I was mad by planning to include two separate walks within the same day, I was happy to find that other walkers do the same thing! In this instance I was glad that I had a companion to chat to, for my temporary walking chum shared my enthusiasm for the fells, he having only eleven Wainwrights to go before completion. Driving around to the car park at Overbeck Bridge, we parked up and began the gruelling ascent.

Yewbarrow is a fell that both nightmares and dreams are made of. Thankfully this walk was formed out of the latter rather than the former. Like a sleeping dragon lying provocatively on the ground, Yewbarrow's domed form captivates my eye every time I glance along Wasdale. I had read about dramatic climbs and the difficult ascent and was eager to encounter these for myself. Today would be the day. From the very start of the climb, I reached the conclusion that Yewbarrow was one of the best fells in the *Pictorial Guides*. Brilliant scrambling, scree-filled paths, near-vertical ascents, wondrous views – Yewbarrow has these and more all tied up in a neat little package. I came upon the astonishing feature of Great Door unexpectedly, and it took my breath away. I visited both summits, and raved about the views and the mountain. For a fell that is only a little over two thousand feet high, Yewbarrow boasts more excitement than many of the bigger mountains. The descent over Stirrup Crag was equally as thrilling, as hands were needed to climb carefully down the mountainside. At Dore Head I parted ways with my fellow hiker, he going on to claim Red Pike whilst I strolled back to the car park. Yewbarrow, you were one of the most exciting mountains in all of the two hundred and fourteen. Give yourself a pat on the back, my friend. To conclude the day, I paddled in Wastwater and cooled my hot feet, all the while watching the sunshine on the rippling water and gazing up at the mighty Yewbarrow. With only three fells to go, I felt invincible.

One of my three remaining fells was the second highest mountain in England, Scafell, yet I did not want Scafell to be my final Wainwright. During the countdown from fourteen to one (which sounds suspiciously similar to a much-loved television game show) I had

Great Door on Yewbarrow

thought much about the mountain which would take the crown and be hailed as the culmination of my journey. Scafell, though a worthy contender, has too much pizzazz. I favoured a lesser-known fell which instilled as much admiration, awe and ambition in the beholder as Scafell. After much, deliberation, I had made my choice. Nevertheless, Scafell still needed to be climbed, and climb it I did.

I plotted my route carefully to include two thirds of my remaining Wainwrights – Slight Side and Scafell. The tiny car park opposite Wha House Farm was selected as my starting point, and the Brackenclose car park in Wasdale my end point. I employed my trusty and willing chauffeur to collect me at the end of the day, applied liberal amounts of sun cream (today was going to be a scorcher), waved goodbye to the eager farmhouse dogs, and set off along the Terrace Route to Slight Side. Meandering routes and easy gradients make for sublime, carefree walking, and I all but danced along the path. With no companions except sheep, I saw nobody until I encountered the steep and rough pull up to the summit of Slight Side. Surprisingly, as I approached the top, a walker emerged from the side of me, three metres ahead. This simply would not do. I was determined to be the first hiker on the summit of Slight Side that day, and could not bear the thought that another would beat me to it. There was only one thing for it. I gritted my teeth, attached small rocket launchers (available from all good outdoors shops) to the heels of my much abused walking boots and hurtled up the fell with grim determination, hearing gasps of shock from the aforementioned rogue walker as two streaks of flame whizzed up the mountainside. On a more realistic note, I merely upped my pace, passed the usurper with a jaunty "Good Morning!" and clambered onto the rocky summit before him. The extra exertion paid off, though. I was the first hiker on Slight Side that day, and boy did it felt good. Pointy and sharp, Slight Side is a satisfying summit that is often ignored in favour of his larger neighbour, and I confess that my eyes, too, were drawn to my penultimate fell.

In the distance, mountain number two hundred and thirteen beckoned. Like a magnet to iron filings, Scafell drew me closer, and I reverently stepped down from Slight Side and began the walk by the cliff edges to the summit of the second highest mountain in England. The walk between Slight Side and Scafell was uneventful, but it was dramatic, with a raw brilliance that only the Scafell massif can display. I stood proudly next to Scafell's summit cairn, alone for a few blissful minutes, and grinned to myself. This is indeed the life. One of the best aspects of Scafell is that, despite being only fifty feet or so shorter than his bigger brother Scafell Pike, Scafell receives only a tiny fraction of the visitors that Scafell Pike does. As a walker who enjoys her solitude, this puts Scafell streets ahead of Scafell Pike any day of the week. I spoke to a few other discerning walkers who congratulated me on my imminent completion. Despite the sunshine, three thousand feet up in the sky it was quite chilly, and I contemplated my next move. I was well ahead of schedule, and quickly made up my mind to add a short detour to my itinerary, and nip up to the summit of Scafell Pike, as you do.

The descent to Foxes Tarn (Foxes Puddle, more like) was deceptively steep and filled with rolling scree. Once down, there was no option but to begin the tortuous climb up towards the Mickledore ridge. I have long had a fascination with Mickledore and have often wanted to walk between Scafell and Scafell Pike. As such, I grabbed my chance when I could, and it didn't disappoint. Passing rock climbers on the way up, I sat on the narrow ridge and watched activity milling all around me. Hikers strolled past. Climbers roped up. Adventurous sorts tentatively moved through the narrow chute of Lord's Rake to the summit of Scafell. A few agile bodies nimbly scaled Broad Stand and disappeared in amongst the rock face. Ah, Broad Stand. Warned off even attempting it by my parents (with good reason), it is a quick route from the ridge to Scafell, but is definitely more suited to rock climbing with harnesses and ropes and other complicated bits of equipment than for walking boots alone. The poet Samuel Taylor Coleridge inadvertently climbed down Broad Stand during bad weather, and was terrified. With this in mind, I was content to stroll up and look at the opening to the fabled climb, appropriately named 'Fat Man's Agony'. After comparing my figure to the narrow crack in the stone and deciding that I could probably fit through it if I really wanted to, I turned around and made my way to the summit of the highest mountain in England, for the second time that year.

It was a mistake. Scafell Pike was chaos. Hundreds of people in all garbs were milling around the summit. Jeans, shorts, dresses, and lurid tracksuits paraded themselves on top of the main cairn. Portable music players blared ugly music into the atmosphere – the serene calm of lonely mountains could certainly not be found here! To top it all off, a group of youths were selling beer on the summit. I kid you not – they had a keg and everything. Despite the alcohol sales being in aid of charity, I was greatly saddened to see the same plastic beer cups which they were selling lying forlornly in crevices between stones, abandoned immediately after they had served their purpose. Crisp packets and chocolate bar wrappers also littered the summit, and I sincerely hope that those who sold the items were prepared to remove everything that they had brought, and more besides. My only consolation is that they only do this to poor Scafell Pike because he is the highest mountain in England. Thankfully, the rest of the fells are usually left well alone. I removed myself from the summit within approximately twenty seconds of arriving, and retreated back to Mickledore, descending to Wasdale by way of Hollow Stones and Lingmell Gill. Today's message from the mountains had been both powerful and poignant.

Throughout these pages there have been highs and there have been lows, but now there was only one. I had only one fell left which, when conquered, would signify the culmination of my grand plan to climb every single one of the two hundred and fourteen fells featured in Alfred Wainwright's *Pictorial Guides*. Congratulations go to those conscientious readers who have not peeked ahead to see which mountain I saved until last, and are now racking their brains to recall which chosen one is to be my final fell. The wait is over. I wanted a mountain which was in an iconic location, which had an ascent route that could been seen from ground level almost all the way to the top, and which would be memorable. Kirk Fell, you were all that and more. Kirk Fell, over two and a half thousand feet of mountain which would sum up all that I had striven to achieve over the past two hundred and thirteen fells, namely a greater knowledge and understanding of the Lake District. I also liked the fact that, like Wainwright, I would be finishing with a mountain featured in *The Western Fells*, albeit a different one. Die-hard enthusiasts (and perceptive readers) will be able to tell me which of *The Western Fells* was the final one Wainwright explored (it was Starling Dodd, if you were curious).

Kirk Fell. An early start saw the sun rise over Wasdale as I laced up my boots for the final time in my quest. The whole family were here too – Mum, Dad, and my sister, B. My parents were to watch from the valley floor, whilst B (after much persuasion) accompanied me to the summit. To enable my parents to view as much of the ascent as possible, I had selected the most direct route up Kirk Fell there is. Indeed, the path up Highnose Head to the summit must be the most direct route up a fell in the whole of the Lake District. Already highly suspicious of my intentions, the moment B saw the route (which is clearly visible from the valley) heading straight up the mountain, she expressed doubt. "It's easy", I reassured her, "just a simple walk up a hill." I'm not sure she was convinced. We began the steady plod, each step narrowing the gap between 'almost finished the Wainwrights' to 'finished the Wainwrights'. The path was grassy at first, and steps worn into the fell from thousands of earlier feet provided a convenient steep stairway into the sky. We had frequent rest stops, and admired

Number 214 – Kirk Fell

the tremendous view backwards of Wasdale, Wastwater, and the innumerable higgledy-piggledy dry stone walls.

Then the scree began. Small patches at first, like marbles who rolled down when you brushed them with your boot. B looked nervous, I looked nonchalant. All too swiftly, the 'patches' became the terrain, and we encountered boulders of all shapes and sizes. Footholds were precarious, and I could see The Fear emerge in the corner of B's eyes. The only way was up. We aimed for each tiny piece of grass which we could see, and did not stop. B's eyes became glint of steely determination and despite her obvious discomfort she ploughed up the path, never looking behind her. I provided constant streams of encouragement. For an eternity we crept up the mountainside. For B, unused to climbing mountains, it must have felt like a thankless task. I kicked a rock and it bounced down the fellside, gathering momentum as it rolled. B glared at me from below. Step by step we moved upwards and gradually emerged onto the flattening summit plateau. B expressed her delight at being off the near vertical slopes with a series of grunts. Given time, I'm sure she will forgive me for dragging her up there. Until then, she refers to Kirk Fell as 'Death Mountain' and refuses to go walking with me.

As we approached the summit cairn and shelter I broke into a lumbering run, held my arms high in the air and whooped with joy. I was happy, elated, and joyous all at the same time. B followed behind offering congratulations. I plonked my rucksack down and opened it, drawing forth my treasured copies of *The North-Western Fells*, *The Central Fells*, *The Eastern Fells*, *The Northern Fells*, *The Far-Eastern Fells*, *The Southern Fells*, and *The Western Fells*. I had carried all seven faithful tomes to the summit of my final fell, and was determined to record my triumph with photographic evidence. After they were safely stowed away, I brought out the champagne which had also been carted up the mountain. B produced two champagne flutes, and we toasted Kirk Fell, toasted Alfred Wainwright, and toasted my achievement.

I was that excited I could hardly take in the views, and so it was probably just as well that as we ate our sandwiches and drank our champagne it started raining. However, nothing could dampen my mood today. As we departed in the direction of Kirkfell Crags I waved

Higgledy-piggledy dry stone walls in Wasdale. The builders had hit the bottle before going to work that day

the summit goodbye, kissed the air, and could not stop smiling. The walk was not over yet. As we came to edge of the crags and planned our descent, I saw B's face. "You said the worst was over!" she exclaimed. Let us merely say that I had over exaggerated the ease with which we would saunter down the crags to the Black Sail Pass, and thus return to Wasdale and our waiting parents. As it happened, I descended first, following the path left by countless walkers before us. B brought up the rear, and I mean that literally, she choosing to descend mostly on her bottom as she believed it to be safer, and a distinctly wet and muddy bum was the result. Nevertheless, as we made our way down the pass I have never been prouder of her. Drawing from all my Lake District walking expeditions, the gruelling ascent up the nose of Kirk Fell is one of the most difficult in the whole of the region. The combination of steepness and scree is unparalleled, and made for a fitting conclusion to my epic quest. I worked every step of the way, each step bringing my dream ever closer. Upon returning to the car I received more of the warmest congratulations from my parents, opened more champagne, and partook of a celebratory meal in the Strands Inn in Nether Wasdale. It was over.

Mad dash towards the summit of Kirk Fell – the end is nigh!
Photo by Bryony Matthews

AFTERWORD: TRIUMPH AND TREPIDATION

I begin this afterword with mixed emotions. It's all over. Two hundred and fourteen fells have been climbed. From that point in my life I began referring to walking the Wainwrights in the past tense rather than the present. I am not *walking* them anymore. I have *walked* them. It is a strange sensation. It took me one year and four months to climb each and every fell drawn and described in minute detail by Alfred Wainwright. It feels fantastic. I have developed a thorough knowledge of the Lake District, of its villages, tarns, mountains and roads, which is what I set out to achieve. I can offer advice about mountain walking. I know what clothes to wear and what supplies to carry with me. I can share tales by the fireside of drama and of excitement, and give a knowing glance when people refer to 'this' fell, or 'that' ascent. Therein lies the triumph. Therein also lies the trepidation. I now ask myself a Very Important Question. What do I do now?

Having walked all of the Wainwrights, I have by no means finished with them. To believe that you know everything about the mountains in the *Pictorial Guides* is foolish. Many different routes are described and are deserving of attention, and they can't all be used when completing a round of Wainwrights. I do not intend to complete a second round – at least not right now. I do, however, intend to explore some of the fells and paths which I did not encounter during my quest. Pillar's Shamrock Traverse and Blencathra by Hall's Fell Ridge are at the top of my list, as are Scafell via Lord's Rake, and the Gable Girdle. I have ambitions to summit Bowfell by way of the Climber's Traverse and High Street via the Straits of Riggindale. On a perhaps more gentle note, I believe High Rigg deserves a second, more leisurely exploration, as do Troutbeck Tongue, Loughrigg Fell, and Rannerdale Knotts. I feel the need to reacquaint myself with old friends such as Silver How, and reassure them of my loyalty. These dreams may take a lifetime, but I do not mind.

Mountain walking is a strange hobby. We throw ourselves upon the elements in all sorts of weather, getting soaked, sunburnt and shivery all in the name of enjoyment – and sometimes all in one day! It will therefore come as no surprise that my appetite has been whetted to discover more remote and beautiful areas of the countryside. Moreover, as my attention has been focused entirely on the Lake District, I now want to travel further afield. One phrase has repeatedly cropped up during conversations which I have, thus far, paid little attention to. Now, however, I am feeling the lure of 'long distance walking'. Long distance walking appeals to my desire to walk with a clear purpose, to be able to think and reminisce how 'I did that'. The whole of the country, and indeed the world, opens at your fingertips, at the rustle of a map and at the pointing of a compass.

From the famous names of the Pennine Way, Cleveland Way, Offa's Dyke Path, West Highland Way, South West Coast Path, and the Hadrian's Wall Path to the lesser-known Cumbria Way, Viking Way and the Cape Wrath Trail, I want to walk them all. The only question is where to start! New skills will be learnt, new areas explored, and a knowledge of the Great British countryside gained. Not that I would ever forget the dream which started them all, of course – Wainwright and his seven pocket-sized books. Wainwright also produced *The Outlying Fells of Lakeland*, a collection of walks which feature a number of the lower (but no less worthy) fells in Cumbria, which I hope to begin. However, lurking in the depths of my subconscious is the grandfather to the Wainwrights: the Munros. All two hundred and eighty-four (depending on whether the measuring people change their minds with regards to height) hulking Scottish beasts over three thousand feet tall. More difficult, more of them, further away, harder to reach, harder to climb (indeed the terrifyingly named 'Inaccessible Pinnacle' is classed as a graded rock climb), yet they flit in and out of my mind like a silent movie. It is time to dip my toe out of the comfort blanket which is Lakeland and spread my walking wings.

For now, though, I'm content to flick through photograph albums of blurry summit shots, wash the mud off my abused gaiters and restock my emergency rations, just in case. And yet, I always hear the call of the hills in the distance and the wind sighing for my company. Suddenly I find myself lacing up my faithful walking boots.

I think I'm going to need more maps.

Eleanor Matthews
October 2013

Also from Sigma Leisure:

Wainwright's Secret Lakeland
Volume 1: Northern, North-Western and Central Fells
Chris Stanbury
Volume One of a trilogy designed to cover approximately 200 walks of a secretive and secluded nature in the Lake District covering the Northern, North-Western and Central Fells as defined by Alfred Wainwright. 75 of Wainwright's ascent and ridge routes in Lakeland are described, selected for their secret and secluded nature. The routes are described from a modern perspective with a comparison where appropriate with how Wainwright described them in his day.
£8.99

The World of a Wainwright Bagger
Chris Stanbury
Chris Stanbury provides an insight into the world of a 'Wainwright Bagger', inspiring those new to The Wainwrights, to those who have done most of the fells with a series of essays giving a flavour of the enjoy- ment to be found in completing Wainwright's 214 fells.
£8.99

Nowhere Fast
Walking the Wainwrights
Andy Grigg

The story of one family's attempt to climb all the Wainwights.Climbing over one hundred and ninety five thousand feet (six times the height of Mount Everest), and walking nearly six hundred miles over the course of six years, Nowhere Fast follows the journey of Andy, Tania and their two sons – William and Tom, as they battle the elements and scale the peaks. Sharing success and failure, highs and lows, laughter and tears, the challenge proves that anything is possible and that what really binds a family together is shared experience.
£9.99

Walking the Wainwrights
Stuart Marshall

This book links all 214 peaks in the late Alfred Wainwright's seven-volume Pictorial Guide to The Lakeland Fells. Clear route descriptions are presented with two-colour sketch maps.

"An excellent, concise manual on how to tackle the 'Wainwrights' in an intelligent way." – A. Harry Griffin MBE
£8.99

Railway Walks in the Lake District
Peter Naldrett

This new collection of 20 fabulous Lake District walks enables you to explore the railway heritage of the region, both old and new. Follow the routes from train stations to discover both amazing views and a wealth of information about times gone by. You can learn all about disused lines and stations that stand abandoned following the Beeching Axe of the 1960s. Railway Walks in the Lake District is an engaging and inspirational way to explore Cumbria's wonderful landscape.

£8.99

Walking In Eden
Ron Scholes

The definitive guide to walking in the Eden Valley, a unique part of Cumbria nestling between Kendal and Carlisle. The walks, both circular and linear, range from 2 to 15 miles and are peppered with fascinating accounts of the history and culture of the area. Outline route maps, inspiring photographs and absorbing background information all add to the value of this unique guide to walking in the Eden Valley – the closest that walkers will get to a paradise on earth!

£9.99

Waterside Walks in the Lake District 2nd Ed
Colin Shelbourn

25 stunning walks along the shores of some of the most beautiful lakes to strolls beside rushing rivers and wild water- falls. Whatever the length or location you choose you'll meet with stunning scenery, a richness of wildlife, and many interesting places to visit.
£8.99

Lake District Natural History Walks
Case Notes of a Nature Detective
Christopher Mitchell

18 walks suitable for all ages and abilities Fascinating facts help you interpret the country- side by looking at the effects of geology and plant life on the animal population of the area.
£8.99

35 Really Good Lake District Walks
Peter Bowker

This book describes 35 quality outings in the mountains of the English Lake District. The walks, which all visit at least one 'Wainwright' summit, have been specifically chosen to appeal particularly to those who prefer to travel at a leisurely pace on straightforward routes which avoid more challenging and demanding situations.

£8.99

Lost Lakeland
In the footsteps of Thomas Pennant
Christopher Mitchell

Thomas Pennant was an eighteenth-century travel writer, antiquary and naturalist. Travelling on horseback with a group of friends and servants including his own artist, he was one of the first to explore the Lake Counties. This book follows Thomas Pennant's historic journey. It revisits what has become familiar ground and in the process discovers a 'lost' Lakeland **£8.99**

North Lakeland Walks with Children

Mary Welsh; illustrations by Christine Isherwood

"It has been great fun speaking to children I have met on the walks and listening to what they have to say," says Mary Welsh. Written specifically for parents of reluctant walkers.

£8.99

South Lakeland Walks with Children

Nick Lambert

"With Nick Lambert's lively commentary, there seems little likelihood that recalcitrant children will be bored or fratchy."
– The Keswick Reminder

£8.99

All of our books are all available on-line at **www.sigmapress.co.uk** or through booksellers. For a free catalogue, please contact:

Sigma Leisure, Stobart House, Pontyclerc, Penybanc Road, Ammanford, Carmarthenshire SA18 3HP
Tel: 01269 593100 Fax: 01269 596116

info@sigmapress.co.uk   www.sigmapress.co.uk